PTSD:

A THEOLOGICAL APPROACH

PTSD:

A THEOLOGICAL APPROACH

DR. SCOTT JIMENEZ

XULON ELITE

Xulon Press
2301 Lucien Way #415
Maitland, FL 32751
407.339.4217
www.xulonpress.com

Paperback ISBN-13: 978-1-66286-391-2
Hard Cover ISBN-13: 978-1-66286-392-9
Ebook ISBN-13: 978-1-66286-394-3

ACKNOWLEDGEMENTS

No book is written, edited, published, and marketed without some help. After I read the manuscript for what seemed the 5000th time, I could not tell if the words I was seeing were on the page or in my mind. I would like to thank the following people for clarifying that distinction: Bob Wichtman, Allen Sper, and Leah Faulkes,

The Tom Lea Institute gave me permission to use Tom Lea's painting "That 2000 Yard Stare". This remarkable painting was done following the battle for the island of Peleliu in 1944 in WWII. Tom was a Life magazine correspondent, a civilian imbedded illustrator with the Marine Corps in the Pacific through many of the island-hopping campaigns. His painting of a real Marine, unnamed, shows a battle scene, with the foreground occupied by his face. The eyes are the focus, evocative and haunting. This is the face of battle, of countless mind-numbing experiences that may never be told. For more information, please visit the Tom Lea Institute in El Paso, TX, or go to https://www.tomlea.com to see upcoming events.

I want to thank Texas Graphic Co in Big Spring, TX for seeing Tom Lea's painting, then envisioning and creating the cover art I dreamed of. They may be contacted at: orders@texasgraphicsco.com.

Often behind every doe-eyed writer is someone to keep them on track. I especially want to thank my wife, Gloria, for allowing me to devote a lot of time to this project, while excusing me when my mind was obviously focused elsewhere. She has lived through my struggles, given me wisdom, prayed over me and with me. Her love and her faith have sustained me. Again, thank you, my love.

Finally, the team at Xulon, who put teeth to my desire to write this book. Countless people I have never met, but respect, have guided this project to completion.

TABLE OF CONTENTS

Chapter 1

WHY THIS BOOK?

Matthew 10:28-28 says, "Come to Me, all who are weary and heavy burdened, and I will give you rest. Take my yoke up on you and learn from Me, for I am gentle and humble in heart, and you will find rest for your souls." I think this verse was written for those who suffer, and suffer deeply.

One Veteran[1] I interviewed, that I will call Veteran B, told me, "Even if God could forgive me, I can't forgive myself." This is such a powerful statement he made. His Vietnam wartime experiences were of combat, of unimaginable atrocities, of guilt and shame for participating in some of these events, and of dealing with or of not dealing with forgiveness and unforgiveness. It took a long time to change his perspective on how he perceived God, how God relates to us, and on the true nature of forgiveness. His story, in a nutshell, is the story of many who suffer from traumatic experiences, especially when these experiences were due to combat.

I wrote this book for combat Veterans. This book came out of my experiences while on active duty, both as an officer of

---

[1] I capitalize the word "Veteran" as both a title and to show deep respect for those who have put on a uniform.

Marines and then as a Navy chaplain often serving Marines, combined with my experiences working with Veterans while a VA chaplain.

I mourn for those that did not come home, celebrate with those that did, and minister to those who left something "over there". What was left behind can be physical, relational, emotional, and/or spiritual.

I also wanted to write something for those interested in working with combat Veterans, as well as those unfamiliar with Post Traumatic Stress Disorder (PTSD). There have been discussions whether to keep that label, or to shorten it to Post Traumatic Stress (PTS). Because many people know the term PTSD, I will use that term throughout this book. Veteran S eloquently describes what he went through,

> For me PTSD is not only dealing with experienced trauma, it is also dealing with disappointment. Striving so hard for certain outcomes and being presented with devastating results. PTSD is born in trauma, nurtured in frustration, fostered in disappointment, and grows into self-loathing reclusion. All of this pertains to this world and the experiences we have here as our life unfolds in our fallen state of being. How do we reconcile this? The answer is beyond our selves, the answer is beyond our experience, the answer is in the Lordship of Christ.

I worked with Veterans who had PTSD, sometimes hidden behind Substance Use Disorder (SUD). They would often tell me about their wartime experiences that plagued them.

Chemicals, whether in the form of alcohol or other medications, were an attempt to hold those remembrances of those experiences at bay, if only for a little while, by self-medicating.

I initially did research for a Doctor of Ministry (D.Min) while a Department of Veterans Affairs (VA) chaplain. I did primary research, interviewing combat Veterans, identifying them by letters.: A,B,C, etc., to protect their anonymity. I also did secondary research, which entailed a lot of reading, sifting, and recombining the data found. This recombining was both novel and crucial, as there are neither books nor research focusing on a theological approach to PTSD. I believe that this is a disservice to Veterans, depriving them of a truly holistic approach to their pain. If we do not address the theological underpinnings of a traumatic event, how we see it, how it envelops us, and how we react when trying to integrate the event into our life, then we have not used a holistic approach. By not addressing theology, we cannot find a truly holistic approach. My dissertation, which became the main part of this book, was on finding a holistic approach to PTSD, focusing on faith by incorporating theology. Because this is a new field, I have included several pages of Bibliography and Works Consulted at the end of this book.

Many Veterans use the Twelve Step programs offered through Alcoholics Anonymous (AA) and Narcotics Anonymous (NA). There is a spiritual component inherent in both of these programs. Founded in 1935 by Bill Wilson (Bill W.) and Robert Smith (Dr. Bob), AA started out as an overtly Christian program. It has toned down the language to a more broad-based and generalized (some would say watered-down) spirituality, but when I taught the Twelve Steps, as a chaplain, I emphasized the Christian aspects of each step.

Veterans who have returned to the AA/NA program tell me that if they forego the spiritual component, their recovery won't last. One said, "You have two choices: get spiritual help, or die." Many of these Veterans have admitted to me that they drink or use drugs so they can either not remember or forget something that lies beyond, something traumatic. Another said, "I have nightmares. I drink so I can sleep." The temporary solution to their problem then becomes another problem: substance addiction. Howard Wasdin, a Veteran involved in the battle for Mogadishu, Somalia, which was famously portrayed in the book and movie, *Black Hawk Down*, said, "When you hurt on so many levels, alcohol-induced numbness becomes addictive."[2]

PTSD is pernicious and devastating. Many Veterans suffer throughout their lifetime due to one experienced event. A 2008 telephone study conducted by the RAND Corporation of 1,965 previously deployed Veterans found that 14 percent of them screened positive for PTSD.

The researchers speculate, "Assuming that the prevalence found in this study is representative of the 1.64 million service members who had been deployed for OEF/OIF[3] as of October 2007, we estimate that approximately 300,000 individuals

---

[2] Howard Wasdin and Joel Kilpatrick, *The Last Rescue: How Faith and Love Saved a Navy SEAL Sniper*, (Nashville, TN: Nelson Books, 2014), 76.

[3] OEF refers to Operation Enduring Freedom, U.S. military operations in Afghanistan; OIF refers to Operation Iraqi Freedom, U.S. military operations in Iraq.

currently suffer from PTSD or major depression."[4] While PTSD
is identified as a stress disorder, it is not the same as depression.
Perhaps other studies will look at only PTSD. While acknowledging these differences, the numbers of those suffering from
PTSD can only have increased since that time.

There are many treatment modalities for PTSD that address
some of the issues presented. These are most commonly
addressed from a psychological basis, not a spiritual basis.[5]

And yet, some of the trauma incurred may have its roots
in the spiritual realm, not the psychological. If spirituality is
important for SUD, could it not also be important for a traumatic
event like PTSD? I believe the answer is: yes. The following
pages will show that not only is faith an important element in
PTSD recovery, but that without faith, a true holistic recovery
may not even be possible. Faith then becomes an integral part
of an individual sufferer's recovery. And that is precisely the
point where the Church (all Christian churches) have a say,
have an entry point, and have some of the answers needed (or
at least can point the way to Truth).

All who minister to active duty and reserve military, to
Veterans, and to their families, are in a unique position to serve,
to listen, and to help. Military and VA Chaplains are especially
important as this is their primary field of service, training, and
often, interest. It is also easy to identify with another's reality

---

[4] Terri Tanielian and Lisa H. Jaycox, editors, "Invisible Wounds of War:
Psychological and Cognitive Injuries, Their Consequences, and Services
to Assist Recovery." xxi, http://www.rand.org/content/dam/rand/pubs/
monographs/2008/RAND_MG720.pdf (Accessed November 4, 2014.)

[5] While I am not setting up an adversarial distinction between the bases, I
am merely stating that the basis often forms the approach.

if one is close to that reality. There are times, when as a military chaplain, I had a captive audience: I lived, slept, ate, and played where I worked, as did my parishioners. I was an active duty Marine and later, a Navy Chaplain. I have been deployed and have also been in combat areas. Because I can identify, my role is to listen, and then to guide them to applying their faith to their lives by advocating the very faith they espouse. For some, the goal is to encounter a living, vibrant faith. This has been my parish.

While there have been numerous studies of patients with co-morbid SUD and PTSD, and some have focused on Veterans,[6] it seems the majority have discussed general PTSD. I will argue later that this is not the kind of PTSD many Veterans may be exposed to in combat.[7] If what I have seen in a VA SUD domiciliary (called a dormitory elsewhere) is an indication of the Veteran population, then the trend for co-morbidity seems to be increasing for this population. Still, even though some of these studies do not focus solely on Veterans, the information is interesting and may be applicable to Veterans. Pamela Brown's

---

[6] D. Scott McLeod, et al., "Genetic and Environmental Influences on the Relationship among Combat Exposure, Posttraumatic Stress Disorder Symptoms, and Alcohol Use." *Journal of Traumatic Stress*, 14(2)(2001):259-275.

[7] Joshua Dolan, "Treatment of Dual Diagnosis Post Traumatic Stress Disorder and Substance Use Disorders: A Meta-Analysis." (2012). Marquette University Dissertations (2009 -). Paper 177. http://epublications.marquette.edu/dissertations_mu/177(Accessed September 25, 2014.)

study on women found that targeted treatment for co-morbid PTSD and SUD might benefit both disorders.[8]

Another study by Brown focused solely on relapse, but by women, thereby making the results potentially inapplicable to male subjects.[9] And yet, there have been some promising findings. In another study, Brown says, "When one disorder worsened, the other disorder was more likely to worsen. When one disorder improved, the other disorder was likely to improve as well."[10] This is an indication that these disorders should be treated concurrently, not separately.

This is also a call for more research. Brown reports,

> Traditionally, substance abuse researchers and PTSD researchers have worked in mutually exclusive organizations and programs, have received funding from separate government agencies, and have disseminated their findings in different specialized journals. Clearly, the schism between the two fields must be bridged if we hope to develop effective, integrated,

---

[8] Pamela J. Brown, "Outcome in Female Patients with both Substance Use and Post-Traumatic Stress Disorders. *Alcoholism Treatment Quarterly*, 3, Vol 18, (2000):127.

[9] Pamela J. Brown, Robert L. Stout, and Timothy Mueller, "Posttraumatic Stress Disorder and Substance Abuse Relapse Among Women: A Pilot Study." *Psychology of Addictive Behaviors*, 2, Vol 10, (1996):124- 128.

[10] Pamela J. Brown, Robert L. Stout, and Jolyne Gannon-Rowley, "Substance Use Disorder-PTSD Comorbidity: Patients' Perceptions of Symptom Interplay and Treatment Issues." *Journal of Substance Abuse Treatment*, 5, Vol 15, (1998):447.

comprehensive treatments for patients suffering
from both SUDs and PTSD.[11]

Pastors, ministers, rabbis, and chaplains may encounter, or
have congregations with, Veterans who cross the spectrum of
multigenerational, socio-economic, racial, cultural, gender, and
spiritual/philosophical boundaries, as well as type and severity
of PTSD, length of deployment, type and branch of service, and
type and severity of SUD.

The theme of my book is to give the pastor[12] and any others
who work with Veterans a means of doing so. This can be
done by understanding the processes involved in getting the
Veteran to that point, by knowing one's own limitations, and
by knowing when to refer to appropriate help.

Sometimes it is not headline-grabbing events that bring
attention to a story. Upon coming home from war, I greeted
my wife and kids, then, exhausted, I went to bed. I slept in a
real bed, something I had not done while in the warfront. Here
my memory ends, and my wife's memory takes over, as I have
zero recollection of these events. When she crawled into bed,
she reports that I "stopped breathing, looked over my shoulder,
and said, 'Oh, it's you!'" I had no idea any changes had happened to me. If something that minor was a shock to me, what
else was I not aware of? And if I did not recollect that event,

---

[11] Pamela J. Brown, and Paige C. Ouimette, "Introduction to the Special
Section on Substance Use Disorder and Posttraumatic Stress Disorder
Comorbidity." *Psychology of Addictive Behaviors*, 2, Vol 13, (1999): 77.

[12] Here I include any clergyperson, in a variety of contexts, that work with
and minister to Veterans.

what else was I not recollecting? Sometimes it is in the ordinary that major breakthroughs come.

I will present available research on spirituality, combined with qualitative interviews from a sample of Veterans with PTSD. The subjects were Veterans recruited from public recovery programs for SUD, as there were none locally for PTSD. The parameters used to establish PTSD are included as Appendices B and C.

I will then give suggestions as to how this information may then be utilized by clergy, pastors, and chaplains. My prayer is that neither the Veteran nor the one trying to help them feel alone.

I try to define terms when possible, as psychological, medical, and theological language may use different terms, or even the same term with vastly different meanings. Even in the same field, there are subspecialities. For example, in the medical field, ED may mean the Emergency Department of a hospital, or it can mean Erectile Dysfunction. For an educator, ED may mean Educationally Deficient. And so on.

Even within the military, terms have to be defined, as each military branch has its own particular patois, which may seem confusing to members of other branches. The base retail store in the Marine Corps may be called a Marine Corps Exchange (MCX), while in the Army it may be a Base Exchange (BX). In the Navy, it is a Naval Exchange (NEX), while in the Air Force, it is an Armed Forces Exchange (AFEES).

After I returned from Desert Storm, I resigned my commission in the Marine Corps, went to seminary, and accepted a commission in the Navy as chaplain, and began serving on active duty. Then 9/11 happened. As I listened and ministered to those affected, I found for many the current trauma had some prior unresolved trauma and issues behind it. These past issues would be exacerbated by the current issues, making for a complex recovery. I had to help people with the trauma of 9/11, but often I also had to work through unresolved trauma prior to this event, making for complex trauma, and thus, complex recovery.

After retiring from the Navy, I became a VA chaplain. I worked with PTSD patients who presented with SUD. I learned psychological and medical approaches to PTSD. Beyond a physical necessity, most medical approaches were psychiatric in nature, and that meant a mainly pharmacological approach. Let me be clear: I have the ultimate respect for practitioners of mental health. Nevertheless, I am saying that a spiritual injury requires a spiritual approach to render spiritual healing. And PTSD is a spiritual injury.

I have listed in the pages of this book the body of my experiences, the fruit of my research, and the shared pain of walking alongside someone in pain, as well as a new path to restoration and transformation. This book details my findings and is the sum of my experiences, education, research, inclination, and motivation: in short, my head and my heart.

Since there is some weighty material to wade through in each chapter, I have included a short section at the conclusion of most chapters that I call Take Aways. This is a short summary of the chapter's main points or highlights. It re-emphasizes points I think bear repeating, and puts them together in one paragraph.

For those unfamiliar with AA, I have included the 12 Steps as Appendix A. These steps can be applied to areas other than addiction. And for those wanting to self-assess for PTSD, I have included two instruments: the Burns PTSD Scale located in Appendix B, and the PCL-5 PTSD Checklist located in Appendix B. Both of these are 20-question survey instruments.

One can use these instruments to self-assess, or one can use these instruments to understand better what PTSD is and does to an individual. Taken together, these instruments can be useful tools for those that work, for those that minister, to Veterans who are suffering.

Chapter 2

OPERATIONAL DEFINITIONS

Operational Definitions

Terms can have both psychological and theological meanings. Sometimes they are similar; oftentimes they are not. Some terms may require that I provide my own definition.

PTSD

PTSD is considered a psychiatric disorder. There have recently been discussions about whether to call this Post Traumatic Stress or Post Traumatic Stress Disorder.[13]

In 2013, the American Psychiatric Association (APA) revised the PTSD diagnostic criteria in the fifth edition of its Diagnostic and Statistical Manual of Mental Disorders (DSM-5). While there were changes made throughout the criterions A-G, those most applicable to spirituality involve two criteria:

---

[13] The Department of Defense (DOD) seems to believe that warriors, having gone through combat, may admit to having stress, but feel the labeling of "disorder" as pejorative. The APA and DOD disagree on the title.

Criterion A: Stressors, and Criterion D: Negative alterations. The current diagnostic for these two criteria is specified below:

Criterion A.[14] Exposure to actual death or threatened death, actual or threatened serious injury, or actual or threatened sexual violence in one (or more) following ways:

1. Directly experiencing the traumatic event(s)

2. Witnessing, in person, the event(s) as it occurred to others

3. Learning that the traumatic event(s) occurred to a close family member or close friend was exposed to trauma. In cases of actual or threatened death of a family member or friend, the event(s) must have been violent or accidental.

4. Experiencing repeated or extreme exposure to aversive details of the traumatic event(s), usually in the course of professional duties (e.g., first responders collecting human remains; police officers repeatedly exposed to details of child abuse)

Note: Criterion A4 does not apply to exposure through electronic media, television, movies, or pictures, unless the exposure is work related.

The only change to this criterion is that the DSM-IV noted "The person's response involved intense fear, helplessness, or

---

[14] American Psychiatric Association, *Diagnostic and Statistical Manual of Mental Disorders.* 5th ed. (Arlington, VA; American Psychiatric Publishing, 2013), 271.

horror."[15] This has been removed in the DSM-V. While the DSM-V has been in print since 2013, it takes time for agencies to change paperwork, reporting, and mindset. At the time this paper was written, change was on- going in the VA.

Criterion D[16]: Negative alterations in cognitions and mood associated with the traumatic event(s), beginning or worsening after the traumatic event(s) occurred, as evidenced by two (or more) of the following:

1. Inability to remember an important aspect of the traumatic event(s) (typically due to dissociative amnesia and not to other factors such as head injury, alcohol or drugs)

2. Persistent and exaggerated negative beliefs or expectations about oneself, others, or the world (e.g. "I am bad," "No one can be trusted," "The world is completely dangerous," "My whole nervous system is permanently ruined")

3. Persistent, distorted cognitions about the cause or consequences of the traumatic event(s) that led the individual to blame himself/herself or others

4. Persistent negative emotional state (e.g. fear, horror, anger, guilt, or shame) [trauma- related emotions]

---

[15] American Psychiatric Association, *Diagnostic and Statistical Manual of Mental Disorders.* 4th ed. (Arlington, VA; American Psychiatric Publishing, 2000), 467.

[16] American Psychiatric Association, *DSM-5.*, 271-272.

5. Markedly diminished interest or participation in significant activities [pre- traumatic]

6. Feeling detachment or estrangement from others [alienated]

7. Persistent inability to experience positive emotions (e.g. inability to experience happiness, satisfaction, or loving feelings) [constricted affect]

The criteria for PTSD are not combat-specific, i.e., the stressors can come from events in everyday life unrelated to combat. Simply put, PTSD can be described as "I saw," "I experienced," "I felt." Also, PTSD sufferers vary in their response, their severity, and, ultimately, their recovery, based on many factors, one of which is prior trauma exposure. David Wood reminds us that much of the body's response to danger is a survival tactic, which is a good thing when one is in a survival situation, "Many of the symptoms of post-traumatic stress— nervousness, insomnia, anxiety in crowds, jumping at a sudden loud noise—are primitive, involuntary instincts necessary to survival in a combat zone."[17] But after the situation passes, these same survival skills can hamper function. As Jennifer Vasterling, et al, relate, "All service members must learn skills that are essential, but specific, to survival in a combat environment; these same skills, if not sufficiently adapted, can lead to

---

[17] David Wood, "Iraq, Afghanistan War Veterans Struggle With Combat Trauma", http://www.huffingtonpost.com/2012/07/04/iraq- afghanistan-war-veterans-combat-trauma n 1645701.html. posted 7/4/2012, 6, (Accessed July 9, 2012.)

significant problems upon returning home."[18] This transition, from combat with skills learned leading to survival, to a civilian setting where a new set of skills need to overwrite previous learning, is fraught with stress. Some never make this transition.

For Criterion A, Bruce P. Dohrenwend looked at the roles of three primary factors; severity of combat exposure (e.g., life experiences or traumatic events during combat), pre-war vulnerabilities (e.g., childhood physical abuse, family history of substance abuse) and involvement in harming civilian or prisoners. While the severity of combat exposure was the strongest predictor of whether the soldiers developed PTSD, pre-war vulnerability was just as important in predicting the persistence of the PTSD over time.[19]

Jonathan Shay uses a term that for me differentiates the complex PTSD many combat Veterans have, "combat post-traumatic stress disorder."[20] Combat PTSD may differ from other types of PTSD in that there may be an elevated sense of danger. Jennifer Vasterling tells us, "The battlefield differs from many

---

[18] Jennifer J. Vasterling, Erin S. Daly, and Matthew J. Friedman, "Posttraumatic Stress Reactions Over Time: The Battlefield, Homecoming, and Long-term Closure," ed. Josef I. Ruzek, et al., *Caring for Veterans with Deployment-Related Stress Disorders: Iraq, Afghanistan, and Beyond.* (Washington, D.C.: American Psychological Association, 2011), 40.

[19] Bruce P. Dohrenwend, et al., "The Roles of Combat Exposure, Personal Vulnerability, and Involvement in Harm to Civilians or Prisoners in Vietnam War-Related Posttraumatic Stress Disorder," *Clinical Psychological Science*, 10, Vol 20, (2012): 12-13.

[20] Jonathan Shay, *Achilles in Vietnam: Combat Trauma and the Undoing of Character.* (NY: Simon and Schuster, 1995), xx.

other life-threatening contexts. Dangers often persist for days or months at a time, potentially leading to prolonged stress responses."[21] Responses to stressors are often learned. Virtually every combat Veteran I have talked to has suffered from some form of hyper-vigilance and hyper- alertness, responses forged in the stressors of the heat of battle.

The result? As Edward Tick puts it, "In war, chaos over-whelms compassion, violence replaces cooperation, instinct replaces rationality, gut dominates mind."[22] The responses learned in war do not end when the war ends. Daniel Pitchford elaborates, "War changes people. Even more, a person who experiences war endures the worst of humanity in that he or she must choose to kill or be killed or even to flee so that so-called safety and refuge can be found."[23] Simply put, combat PTSD may have an element of "I did." The difference between "I did," and "I saw", "I experienced", and "I felt" cannot be exaggerated. The element of "I did" implies a commission. It can also imply even an omission "I did not do" as this relates to guilt. While these elements are imbued with a deep emotional impact, the impact goes further into our psyches. Interestingly, this word is from the Greek, referring to the goddess of the

---

[21] Jennifer J. Vasterling, "Posttraumatic Stress Reactions Over Time: The Battlefield, Homecoming, and Long-term Closure," In *Caring for Veterans with Deployment-Related Stress Disorders: Iraq, Afghanistan, and Beyond*, 37.

[22] Edward Tick, *War and the Soul: Healing Our Nation's Veterans from Post-Traumatic Stress Disorder*. (Wheaton, IL: Quest Books, 2005), 16.

[23] Daniel Pitchford, "An Existential Study of Iraq Veterans' Traumatizing Experiences," UMI: 3339401, San Francisco: Saybrook Graduate School and Research Center, 2008, 9.

soul. Taken in this original meaning, these experiences affect the mind and the soul or spirit.

PTSD can happen to anyone, given the right (or wrong) circumstances. It also affects people in unique ways. Their reactions may seem abnormal and may cause them to wonder if that is normal behavior. This tension is explained by Victor Frankl, "An abnormal reaction to an abnormal situation is normal behavior."[24] The one changed remains changed. A return to normalcy is an exercise in futility because the abnormality of experience changes what was once normal; the old normal is no more. The search begins for a new normal.

It may pay to bear in mind what Nigel Biggar said of war and apply it to PTSD, "The danger, however, is that intellectual tidiness with its careful logic, clear concepts, and nice distinctions ceases to do justice to the intractable messiness of flesh-and-blood human experience—that it buys clarity at the expense of reality."[25] The reality is that as war is messy, so also PTSD is messy and may require a variety of approaches from multiple disciplines, a true multidisciplinary team approach. Another reality, as shown in the many criteria for it, is that PTSD sufferers may have both similar and dissimilar experiences. This is also true for depth of trauma, support systems, and successes in recovery.

---

[24] Victor E. Frankl, *Man's Search for Meaning.* (Boston: Beacon Press, 2006), 20.

[25] Nigel Biggar, *In Defence of War.* (Oxford: Oxford University Press, 2014), 4.

Robert Certain seems to agree when he speaks about society providing a "'lifeline' anchored to society's ethical core."[26] He continues, "It is also important that some sort of mechanism be in place to 'reel in the lifeline' when the battle is done. Parades and medals provide a secular answer; confession and absolution provide the religious answer."[27] To go further, the answer may lie in confession and absolution within a community of faith, guided by Scripture, and using the discipline of prayer.

While I do not take issue with these various definitions, I would add that the result of trauma is often manifested in a search for identity. By this I mean that the image of how we see ourselves (immortal, invincible, indestructible, whole, etc.) is often broken. Trauma brings to focus of the reality of mortality, of being wounded, of losing parts (emotional, physical, spiritual). While there are psychological aspects of this, at the root these are spiritual questions which will be explored in later chapters. I believe the answer to this question of identity, a search for a self-image after a traumatic event can best be answered theologically, in faith, to and by a loving God.

SUD

It has already been mentioned that Veterans may have co-morbid disorders. SUD is one that is presented frequently. SUD has several elements involved. The DSM-5 tells us, "The essential feature of a substance use disorder is a cluster of cognitive, behavioral, and physiological symptoms indicating that

---

[26] Robert Certain, *Unchained Eagle: From Prisoner of War to Prisoner of Christ*. (Palm Springs, CA: ETC Publications, 2003), 275.

[27] Ibid., 275.

the individual continues using the substance despite significant substance-related problems."[28] In other words, the substance itself overwhelms the individual's resources, including the will, to not use.

Having been a chaplain at a substance abuse domiciliary, (a dormitory specifically for in-patient treatment) I have walked alongside patients who had SUD, sometimes PTSD fronted by SUD, and are working through their addiction. I have been a party to their recovery and sometimes their relapse. I have found that without a faith component to their recovery, they will fail, and continue to fail. Why? Simply because the addiction is too great for them to work through on their own power. I will speak more to this in later chapter.

Guilt/Shame

While there is a deeper understanding of these terms, the simplest definition is that guilt is a feeling due to a deed, either a commission or an omission. It is an "I did" or "I have done wrong" moment where one is the actor. Shame is a bit different in that it focuses on the person, an "I am" or specifically, "I am wrong" moment, which affects core identity. These can happen together or independently. More on these terms in Chapter 6: Guilt/Shame.

Spirituality/Theology

Psychology uses the term "spirituality" for belief in something outside the self. Theology ascribes this belief to a belief

---

[28] American Psychiatric Association, *DSM-5*, 483.

in God. As both a Christian and a Christian chaplain, I further ascribe this belief to Jesus Christ, the son of God. For the most part, I will use spirituality and theology interchangeably, unless the difference is acute. Articles expressing the term "spirituality" often use words conveying the present action of God, as someone who values relationship with us. Many of these articles are not written by theo-logians but by psychologists. Perhaps I am trying to marry apples and oranges, or trying to put lipstick on a pig. But because the term is so widespread, it may be difficult to use another term to convey a movement toward God. While psychology ascribes spirituality to an unknown deity or divinity, I ascribe to and name this deity as God, the historic God of the Bible, the God of Abraham, Isaac, and Jacob, and specifically through His Son, Jesus Christ.

Moral Injury/Spiritual Injury/Soul Injury

All of these terms refer to something beyond PTSD that involves deep emotions that is often not treated nor even addressed in most therapies for PTSD. It may involve killing, but it almost always involves guilt and/or shame. Moral injury was the first term that was used to describe active participation (doing something) or passive participation (seeing something) that goes against our moral center. The term has somewhat fallen out of use due to the idea that Veterans would connect moral injury to being immoral, thus balking at the term.

The next term used was spiritual injury. This term reminded us that our spirit was hurting. Some Veterans balked at this, claiming that they were not spiritual. Much of the literature still uses this term, which I report without change. For me, this term refers to two separate events. The first is the wounding of the Holy Spirit, while the second is a wound to our own individual spirit.

The last term is soul injury. This term seems to not have the baggage the other two terms have. And for that purpose, I favor this term. My definition of soul injury is trauma that wounds our soul, which affects our connection to God, which affects our connection to one another. I admit that a wounding of the soul or a wounding of the spirit seem to convey the same thing.

We will discuss these terms in more detail in Chapter 8: Soul Injury.

Chapter 3

CONFESSION

Confession

There are several questions that need to be answered in a discussion about confession. The first one is, how is confession defined? Perhaps it would be easier to begin with the word "confess". What does "confess" mean?

The *American Heritage Dictionary* defines "confess"[29] as a transitive verb:

1. to disclose or acknowledge (something damaging or inconvenient to oneself); admit

2. to acknowledge belief or faith in

    3a. to make known (one's sins) to God or to a priest

    3b. to hear the confession of (a penitent)

---

[29] *American Heritage Dictionary.* 2nd college ed. (Boston: Houghton Mifflin, 1982), 308.

It also includes the use as an intransitive verb:

1. to admit or acknowledge

2. to tell one's sins to a priest

Confession, then, would be the act of confessing. Using the above definition, confession has in this book two different elements:

1) "I have it." This is the admission. This type of confession is the entry point for identifying Veterans with PTSD, where they can be officially diagnosed with the label of PTSD. (They can be self-identified, but then the VA, and by extension, Chaplains Service, does not officially enter into the picture.)[30]

2) "I did it." This is the disclosure. Both of these elements are necessary for healing to occur. Once identified, the Veteran can then relate their story of what transpired. These recollections are sentinel events, a "something happened that I will never forget" experience. These sentinel events may consume one's thoughts. Confessing them can be therapeutic. A burden shared often becomes a burden lifted.

---

[30] The research in this book focuses on both officially diagnosed and self-diagnosed PTSD sufferers.

Additionally, confession often involves relating that confession to a clergy member and, perhaps, making a faith statement. So, all the aspects of the word "confess" may be utilized.

The Bible tells us in James 5:16, "Therefore, confess your sins to one another, and pray for one another so that you may be healed. The effective prayer of a righteous man can accomplish much."[31] This may be difficult. While some may agree that there is sin involved in the events that led to PTSD, others may not agree. Yet, they may agree that all is not well, that something burdens them. Confession, while painful, is necessary to recovery. Confession, then, may be used to lighten the load that burdens by sharing with someone who will listen in a caring, supportive way. I do not want to lessen the theological importance of confession. Confession is to God. We humans are the visible representation and bestower of what God can accomplish through confession: absolution.

Alcoholics Anonymous (AA) uses a spiritual form of confession, especially in Step 4 and Step 5. Members are to "make a searching and fearless moral inventory of ourselves" (Step Four); and "admit to God, to ourselves, and to another human being the exact nature of our wrongs." (Step Five).[32] Mental health professions are valuing and discussing the role of faith in mental health. Recently the VA has had several conferences on "Bridging Mental Health and Chaplaincy" and produced videos on that subject. Simon Dein tells us, "The evidence suggests that, on balance, religious involvement is generally

---

[31] *New American Standard Bible (NASB)*, (Lockman Foundation, 1995), James 5:16. (All biblical quotations used in this paper are from the NASB, unless otherwise noted.)

[32] Alcoholics Anonymous, *Twelve Steps and Twelve Traditions*, (NY: Alcoholics Anonymous World Services, Inc., 2009), 6.

conducive to better mental health."[33] He continues, "A person's strong religious beliefs may facilitate coping with existential issues whereas those who hold weaker beliefs may demonstrate heightened anxiety."[34] He suggests that mental health "... therapists must endeavor to understand the patient's worldview and, if necessary, consult with clergy."[35] Since one's worldview often reflects their faith, then therapists must seek to understand the patient's faith that impacts on the therapy.

Working with SUD Veterans, I have found that many combat Veterans who self-medicate do so in order to temporarily forget and/or to temporarily not remember certain memories. PTSD may be centered in, and a result of, those memories.

Individual Confession

Confession can be made to one person or to the church. For individuals, Martin L. Smith tells us, "Only the act of bringing everything out into the full light of day in the presence of another will suffice to bring release and relief, the assurance of really handing over sin to God."[36] George Bowman reminds us, "It is God against whom sin has been committed and it is

---

[33] Simon Dein, "Religion, Spirituality, and Mental Health: Theoretical and Clinical Perspectives," *Psychiatric Times*, 1, Vol 27, (January 2010): 1.

[34] Ibid., 3.

[35] Ibid., 5.

[36] Martin L. Smith, *Reconciliation: Preparing For Confession in the Episcopal Church*. (Cambridge, MA: Cowley Publications, 1985), 22.

God who clears the guilt and forgives the sinner."[37] Obviously, Bowman ties confession to sin. I must note that I have spoken with Veterans who feel guilt but may not agree with the concept that they have sinned.[38] And yet they feel guilt. This guilt may be a desire for restoration. Restoration to what? It is a restoration to normalcy, to God, to self-image, to identity, to innocence, and/or to the past. This desire for restoration can only come about because something is broken, and that something is often a negative view of self. Many times this is relational, self in regard to something else, someone else, or the Other. This negative view of self in regard to God is something that will be addressed later in another chapter, under the heading "Guilt". Brokenness does not necessarily have to be sin, but rather, a disruption of the familiar based on one or several sentinel events that may be or are life-changing.

Some individuals may prefer private confession over public or corporate confession. A preference for private confession, David Belgum informs us, is due to, "The plea for privileged communication and the secrecy of private confession is due to the rejection, which to the sinner seems inevitable, were the congregation to know his true nature."[39] If we regard the one who confesses as disabled, then, "A truly functional confession aims at restoring the disabled's integrity and self-regard, returning him to the community from which he has alienated

---

[37] George W. Bowman III, *The Dynamics of Confession.* (Richmond, VA: John Knox Press), 1969, 24.

[38] Sin is a theological term and needs to be introduced here, but it is not a condemnation of individuals for the impossible situations the military often puts them in, often through no fault of their own.

[39] David Belgum, *Guilt: Where Psychology and Religion Meet.* (Englewood Cliffs, NJ: Prentice-Hall, 1963), 13.

himself, and to loving service in holy stewardship of the life God has given him."[40]

Corporate Confession

While confession can be personal, on a one-to-one basis,[41] it can also be corporate. Aaron Murray–Swank, et al., tells us that, "Spiritual confession, when it is practiced in a group or between two individuals, is likely to promote a sense of connectedness through the expression of personal sinfulness in a shared context of beliefs and value regarding sin."[42] One method for dealing with this is a Service/Sacrament/Rite of Reconciliation. Many high liturgical churches (e.g., Catholics,[43] Orthodox,[44] and Episcopalians[45]) have this rite or sacrament. Other churches, like the Church of the Nazarene, have this as a suggested rite, called a Service of Reconciliation.[46]

---

[40] Ibid., 140-141.

[41] Jim Forest, *Confession: Doorway to Forgiveness.* (Maryknoll, NY: Orbis Books, 2002), xiv.

[42] Aaron B. Murray-Swank, Kelly M. McConnell, and Kenneth I. Pargament, "Understanding Spiritual Confession: A Review and Theoretical Synthesis," *Mental Health, Religion, and Culture,* 3, Vol 10, (May 2007): 284.

[43] Donal O. Cuilleanain, *A Guidebook for Confession: The Sacrament of Reconciliation.* (Princeton: Scepter Publishers, 1996), 10-11.

[44] Jim Forest, xii-xvi.

[45] Book of Common Prayer, http://www.bcponline.org, 457-452. (Accessed March 23, 2013.)

[46] Jesse C. Middendorf, *Church Rituals Handbook.* 2nd ed. Church of the Nazarene, (Kansas City: Beacon Hill Press, 2009), 202-210.

The Catholic Sacrament of Reconciliation "(also known as Penance, or Penance and Reconciliation) has these three elements: conversion, confession and celebration."[47]

A chaplain friend instructed me that this should be modified to: contrition, confession, penance, absolution. Contrition is a sincere sorrow for having offended God. Confession is confronting sin by speaking it aloud to a priest. Penance is reparation for our sins. Abso-lution is where a sinner is reconciled to Christ through the merits of the Cross.

Admission of the pain is a confession, of sorts, or at least an initial movement toward the actual precipitating causes. Public articulation of the pain can then lead to finding meaning through the pain. This can often find expression in the public sense. In this public sense, Walter Brueggemann speaks of embracing rather than eradicating, managing, or even tolerating pain. To embrace the pain, not just on an individual level, but on a corporate and communal level, means a "public processing of pain."[48] It is this public articulation of pain that leads to the public processing of pain that is necessary for the individual to release the pain. Shay addresses this when discussing recovery. Using Homer's *The Illiad* as a reference point, and the main character Achilles as a model, Shay argues, "… that healing from trauma depends upon communalization of that trauma…."[49] When a community can embrace the pain, then the community can assist the individual to begin the healing process.

---

[47] "The Sacraments: Reconciliation," http://www.americancatholic.org/features/special/default.aspx?id=32 accessed March 23, 2013.

[48] Walter Brueggemann, *Hope Within History*. (Westminster: John Knox Press, 1987), 16.

[49] Jonathan Shay, xx.

It is also this public articulation of pain that begins to foster hope. Brueggemann continues, "… Hope emerges among those who publicly articulate and process their grief over their suffering."[50] This hope leads to a rebuilding of faith. The faith community empowers the individual to acknowledge and rise above the pain. Because of this, Brueggemann can say, "All faithful theology begins in pain."[51] Perhaps this is due to a questioning of the pain and a seeking of answers. The search for answers, for theological answers, may be rooted in pain.

While Brueggemann sees suffering as theological, Frankl sees suffering as existential, "To live is to suffer, to survive is to find meaning in the suffering. If there is a purpose in life at all, there must be a purpose in suffering and in dying."[52] I would add that while we can acknowledge that there is a meaning to suffering, we should also realize that we may never find that meaning. Perhaps this is why Frankl titled his book, *Man's Search for Meaning.* For the believer and faith practitioner, faith, at its deepest, is not about understanding. Faith is about acceptance, and about obedience, perhaps especially when and because we do not understand.

Take Aways

Confession is both an admission, "I have it", and a disclosure, an "I did it". Confession is necessary for healing for addiction. Could confession be necessary for healing from PTSD? In my experience, yes!

---

[50] Walter Brueggemann, *Hope Within History*, 84.

[51] Ibid., 114.

[52] Victor E. Frankl, 11.

Chapter 4

SURRENDER

Surrender

Christopher Dyslin connects confession with spiritual surrender. He says, "I propose here that the confession of sin to another person is the active ingredient in spiritual surrender, a pride-destructive force, as well as a chief venue of grace."[53] Confession, then, leads to willful surrender. Dyslin continues, "As one surrenders spiritually, that willingness reflects an increasing acceptance of the truth about the limitations of human power and control and growing recognition of reality regarding the ultimate source of power."[54] AA recognizes that growth only comes through surrender. Step Three says, "Made a decision to turn over our will and our lives to the care of God as we understood Him."[55] This echoes what is

---

[53] Christopher W. Dyslin, "The Power of Powerlessness: The Role of Spiritual Surrender and Interpersonal Confession in the Treatment of Addiction," *Journal of Psychology and Christianity,* 1, Vol 27, (Spring 2008): 49.

[54] Ibid., 43.

[55] Alcoholics Anonymous, 5.

said in James 4:7, "Submit therefore to God. Resist the devil and he will flee from you."

Surrender has connotations as well as denotation. Military members are taught to never surrender. The United States Military Code of Conduct, Rules for Prisoners of War, Article II says, "I will never surrender of my own free will. If in command, I will never surrender the members of my command while they still have the means to resist." This can be found under many sources on-line. I used the Army Study Guide.[56]

This seemingly creates a tension between what the Bible says and what the military says. However, the word "surrender" in the Code of Conduct refers to human, earthly institutions. Conversely, when the Bible discusses surrendering or submitting, it is to God.

Veteran B agrees, even though he has trouble relinquishing the past,

> Pain is inevitable; misery is optional. I have a lot of self-induced misery…. I know I can't change the past. I have to let it go. It's easy to say that. I can't let it go. Yet, the only way I know I'm gonna have any peace with it, is to let God take it. Only God can straighten it out. The only way to have peace is to put it in God's hands, let him carry the burden, the memory.

While submitting to God is a spiritual matter, the effects of this submission to God does cross over into our present reality.

---

[56] Army Study Guide, https://www.armystudyguide.com/content/army_board_study_guide_topics/code_of_conduct/the-code-of-conduct.shtml accessed September 1, 2022

The passage in James 4:7 listed above is a prime example. The second part of that verse reads, "Resist the devil and he will flee from you." If we are to be completely honest with ourselves and others, we have tried to resist the devil…and we have failed. The same goes for resisting our baser instincts. For some people, the resistance is against alcohol, drugs, gambling, pornography, etc. We have tried on our own power to resist whatever it is that holds us hostage, and have failed, miserably. The reality is that we have no power to resist the Evil One, Satan, the Devil. It is only when we include the first part of the verse, "Submit therefore to God," that we find power. When I give up my power, I find I have God's power to resist the things I need to resist: Satan, myself, and addictions. Submitting or surrendering my will is a win-win decision. If I give up my pride and my weakness, then I can get power to be healed. Seems like a good trade.

For those that think, or like to think, that they are in control, and that giving up control signifies weakness, let me ask some questions. Are you in control of cancer, of traffic conditions, of other drivers, or of weather patterns? The answer is a resounding 'No!"

To think we are actually in control of our lives is a misreading of reality. We cannot control what we cannot control, and that list is mind-numbing. My weaknesses are that I have no power to resist Satan, in not admitting that I have no power, and in not submitting to Someone, God, who has that power to resist.

I have seen many who have PTSD who are actually out of control. Their relationships are a testimony to this. Being out of control often leads to anger issues, which we will deal with in a later chapter. For those that are in this category, let me say that it does get better with time, if we surrender and submit to God.

Take Aways

Surrender, or submission, goes against our human nature and military training. But, surrender is necessary to recovery from substance abuse. It may follow that it may be necessary for PTSD recovery. In my experience, it is. We each have a choice whether to submit or not.

Chapter 5

REPENTANCE

Repentance

Much of the literature dealing with confession refers to something that happens after, namely repentance. Smith tells us, "… repentance is not just regret for past wrong-doing but a change of heart, a change of direction, a matter of conversion or reconversion to God."[57]

The Bible tells us in Acts 26:20 that repentance is a turning to God, "… that they should repent and turn to God…." This passage continues that this repentance leads to "… performing deeds appropriate to repentance," to "… do works worthy of repentance,"[58] and to "… do deeds consistent with repentance."[59] It also says earlier in Acts 11:18 that, "… repentance that leads to life."

Repentance, then, is not just an intellectual assent of wrong-doing but an active quest to do good works. It is not so much

---

[57] Martin L. Smith, 21.

[58] *Holman Christian Standard Bible (HCSB),* Holman Bible Publishers, 2009, Acts 26:20.

[59] *New Revised Standard Version Bible (NRSV),* National Council of the Churches of Christ in the United States of America, 1989, Acts 26:20

a matter of the mind as it is one of the heart. It is seeing that bad deeds have negative consequences, while good deeds have positive effects. This stems not so much from duty as it does from desire.

We will discuss later the concept that changing the mind, how we *see* things, changes behavior, how we *do* things. Here we want to explore our thoughts. But there is another concept at play of moving from head to heart. It is a process of ingraining our thoughts into our desires, and that changes us. Here we want to explore our hearts. If I no longer have the desire to drink, then I probably will not drink. If I no longer live to please others, an unattainable ideal, then I can live for myself. The Bible passages above tell us there is a greater good, a higher power, God, to live for, something beyond myself.

Chapter 6

GUILT/SHAME

Guilt/Shame

C riterion D in the DSM-5 is about "negative alterations in cognitions and mood that began or worsened after the traumatic event."[60] Symptom #3 specifically deals with blame: "Persistent distorted blame of self or others for causing the traumatic event or for resulting consequences."[61] Confession as concerning PTSD may begin with guilt or shame.[62] This is consistent with many of the feelings associated with PTSD. Ashwin Budden reports, "In studies surveying a range of traumatic stressors, a small but significant percentage of people diagnosed with PTSD report feelings of shame and anger at the most intense moments of the traumatic events rather than fear

---

[60] American Psychiatric Association, *DSM-5*, 271.

[61] Ibid., 272.

[62] While there is a difference between guilt and shame, for the purposes of this book, there will be no distinction. The difference is mainly one of doing or having been done against: in guilt, one is acting, "I have done wrong" (deed); in shame, one is being acted upon, "I am wrong" (core identity). Many Veterans feel both shame and guilt.

and terror."[63] Shame and guilt affect both how PTSD is viewed (as a stress disorder or as an identity disorder or recovery disorder) and how it is treated.

Let me go back to Chapter 2 where we discuss guilt and shame. The simplest definition is that guilt is a feeling due to a deed that I either did (a commission), or I failed to do (an omission). It is an "I did" or "I have done wrong" moment, where one is the actor. Shame is a bit different in that it focuses on the person, an "I am" or specifically, "I am wrong" moment, which affects core identity. Guilt and/or shame are subjects that may be the foundation for the desire to confess.

Guilt is referred to in different ways. Smith declares, "Carrying painful, unhealed memories, self-mistrust or bitter shame uses up the energy and attention that ought to be available for living in the present and meeting its challenges."[64] Bowman tells us, "To face guilt is to face self."[65] Often, a Veteran may come face-to-face with his/her moral center. Murray-Swank, et al., say, "…guilt is an internal signal that shapes relationship- enhancing behavior."[66] The result? There is a difference between what was normative behavior and what is now normative behavior. Sometimes this includes a search for this "new normal." A Department of Veterans Affairs (VA) pamphlet tells us,

---

[63] Ashwin Budden, "The Role of Shame in Posttraumatic Stress Disorder: A Proposal for a Socio- Emotional Model for DSM-V," *Social Science and Medicine*, Vol 69, (2009): 1033.

[64] Martin L. Smith, 34.

[65] George W. Bowman, 71.

[66] Aaron B. Murray-Swank, 283.

These experiences can sometimes lead to long-lasting difficult spiritual and moral questions. The result may be loss of faith, increased guilt and self-blame, and alienation from other people and from God. Individuals may experience a disconnection between these beliefs they were raised with, their expectations about what military service would be like, and their actual war-zone experiences.[67]

False Guilt

While guilt and shame are real and need to be explored, many of the Veterans I saw dealt with a false sense of guilt. This false guilt was due to training, or rather, improper training.

Sometimes this tension is exacerbated by theologians and may cause further guilt. Richard Hays, in his chapter "Violence in Defense of Justice," asks the question, "Is it appropriate for those who profess to be followers of this gentle Shepherd to take up lethal weapons against enemies?"[68] Throughout his book, he lays a foundation for his response, so it is no great wonder what that response would be. His exegesis of the New Testament leads him to not allow violence in any form, even when in defense of those who are vulnerable, or unprotected,

---

[67] "Spirituality and Trauma: Professionals Working Together," Department of Veterans Affairs, National Center for PTSD. Washington, D.C. http://www.ptsd.va.gov/professiona/pages/fs-spiritualtiy.asp, 2,(Accessed January 25, 2013.)

[68] Richard B. Hays, *The Moral Vision of the New Testament.* (NY: Harper Collins, 1996), 317.

or infirm, or young, or old. Further, to engage in violence is un-Christian. Therefore, a Christian can't be involved in war. He seems to imply that soldiers are sinners, simply because they are soldiers. This is not an uncommon sentiment that I have personally encountered in churches, denominational meetings, and seminaries.

Nigel Biggar refutes this by emphasizing that we all sin by our natures; not by the vocation: "On no occasion does it (the New Testament) suggest that a soldier's salvation involves the renunciation of military service as such."[69] Being a soldier is not a sin in itself.

In Matthew 8:5-13 (also Luke 7:1-10), Jesus encounters an unnamed centurion. In 8:10, we read, "Now, when Jesus heard this, He marveled and said to those who were following, 'Truly I say to you, I have not found such great faith with anyone in Israel.'" And in Acts 10: 1-31, we find Peter who encounters, "… Cornelius, a centurion, a righteous and God-fearing and well-spoken of by the entire nation, all the Jews …." If there was ever an opportunity by Jesus and Peter to emphasize Hays' views and decry the profession of arms, these two are it. They do not do so, but instead praise the soldiers' faith.

We are all sinners, by nature, by commission, and by omission. Biggar goes on to note that if military service is not incompatible with Christian discipleship it must be compatible, "then we must infer that it (the New Testament) has no objection in principle to the publicly authorized use of lethal force."[70] The New Testament does not argue that the soldier's profession is evil, nor that the individual is either. Beyond those parameters,

---

[69] Nigel Biggar, 41.

[70] Ibid., 42.

the use of deadly force will be addressed in succeeding paragraphs. Biggar calls those who believe that pacifism is the only response to Christ as "morally inconsistent", saying pacifists "…keep their hands clean only because others are required to get them dirty."[71]

These two responses can add to or detract from guilt, and therefore important. The viewpoint of Hays adds guilt to a situation that may already be, or potentially be, volatile, filled with remorse, and leading to despair. Biggar's response removes the guilt from being a warrior. Simply killing, then, is not unchristian: "Soldiers, whatever their nationality, are not murderers, but executioners."[72] While this distinction may be lost on some, for the warrior the distinction is clear. Biggar speaks of the "double effect" of the agent's intention and the reflexive impact, "Good effects I may intend, but evil effects I may accept only as a side effect."[73] The result may be killing, but not murder, "Morally speaking, deliberately to cause death in this fashion is not the same as intending to kill."[74]

Killing and Murder

How the individual views the distinction between murder and killing may hinge on what the Bible says about taking a life. And this, in turn, depends on the version of the translation. The commandment from God, as expressed in the Ten Commandments as found in Deuteronomy 5:17 says, "You

---

[71] Ibid., 43.

[72] Ibid., 82.

[73] Ibid., 93-94.

[74] Ibid., 101.

shall not murder." This wording in the *New American Standard Bible* is the same in most translations, some of which include the *New Revised Standard Version*[75] and the *Holman Christian Standard Bible.*[76] The exception is the *King James Version* in that it says, "Thou shalt not kill."[77] If the majority translations are correct, then even the Bible, and therefore, God, differentiates between killing and murder. U.S. laws are based on the Ten Commandments, so we as a society also make a distinction between killing and murder.

To go further, in Hebrew, there is a difference between unlawful taking of life, חצ תר (*ratzah*), as found in Exodus 20:13 and Deuteronomy 5:17, and of lawful taking of life, הצ ג (*harag*), as found in Exodus 32: 27-28. To conjoin the two Exodus passages, Moses is on the mountain receiving both the spoken word and the written word (the Ten Commandments) of God. He has been there for almost fifty days when God suddenly tells him in Exodus 32: 7 to "Go down at once!" When Moses gets to the encampment, he sees their sin, calls the people, and says, as recorded in Exodus 32:27-28, "Thus says the Lord, the God of Israel, 'Every man of you put his sword upon his thigh, and go back and forth from gate to gate in the camp, and kill every man his brother, and every man his friend, and every man his neighbor.'" Notice that Moses said, "God says." Since Moses was in the very presence of God and heard the voice of God speak, he knew what He said. Is Moses guilty of breaking this particular commandment, or is there a distinction between killing and murder?

---

[75] *New Revised Standard Version Bible (NRSV)*, Deuteronomy 5:17.

[76] *Holman Christian Standard Bible (HCSB)*, Deuteronomy 5:17.

[77] *King James Version (KJV)*, Public Domain, Deuteronomy 5:17.

If there is a distinction between killing and murder, then feelings of guilt may at times actually be false guilt. One way to see the difference is to remember and acknowledge that upon accepting God's forgiveness, God forgives, but also forgets, as found in Hebrews 10:17, "And their sins and their lawless deeds I will remember no more." If one accepts God's forgiveness on Monday, if then on Tuesday one feels guilt for the same act, then it is certainly not from God but is false guilt sent from Satan.

Take Aways

Guilt is something I did. Shame is something I am. Both may be present at the same time. Sometimes we suffer false guilt by training or by ignorance. Ignorance can be cured by education. One of these areas may be in the distinction between killing and murder. Even the Bible differentiates this difference. For recovery from PTSD, we need to know this distinction well and apply it to our past, as well as our present and future actions.

Chapter 7

IDENTITY

Identity

K ent Drescher reports that this tension affects our thoughts, and, "Our thoughts can be erroneously deceptive, at times."[78] He explains that changing our thoughts is not easy, "Our thoughts are less under control than our behavior."[79] But going further, he says that all is not lost, "Our behavior ultimately influences our thinking, our judgment of who we are."[80] He asks, "Who am I? What say do I have in that process?"[81] And we can shape that process. He says, "Our identity is shaped by our actions. If we want to become a certain person, we have to act like that person."[82] We have a say in that development process of who we are to become. A saying in AA is "I am not who I was, and not yet who I will become." Many of the

---

[78] Kent D. Drescher, telephonic interview by author, National Center for PTSD, Menlo Park, CA, February 8, 2013.

[79] Ibid., interview.

[80] Ibid., interview.

[81] Ibid., interview.

[82] Ibid., interview.

Veterans I encounter confuse the activity with the self. Another saying that cuts to the heart of this is, "I am not my addiction." Another comment heard is, "My past defines me." I counter with, "If your past defines you, your past confines you." Bring that past into the present. We are more than what we do. We are more than our failures or our successes. We are even more than the sum of our parts. And we do have a choice and a voice in who we are to become.

Absolution

Smith believes the remedy is "…the grace of absolution. This grace is the actual release from guilt…."[83] Guilt can happen apart from an acknowledgement of sin. Sin is not necessary for guilt to happen. The goal is to relieve the guilt. Murray-Swank adds, "… many people viewed confession as an initial step to forgiveness and reconciliation with God, resulting in a decrease of guilt and anxiety."[84] Confession is the road to absolution, an acceptance of both God's forgiveness, and of one's own. Confession is not necessarily an admission of sin; it may be more of the feeling one has about something. Sometimes the confession is simply, "I feel guilt." Since many people admit to feeling guilt, to not admit that there is guilt brings its own problems. Forest reminds us, "…a sure symptom of moral death is not to feel guilty."[85] I would add, "If there is a reason to feel

---

[83] Martin L. Smith, 21.

[84] Aaron B. Murray-Swank, 281.

[85] Jim Forest, 6.

guilty." And if there is a reason to feel guilt, to then deny the guilt is to deny the grace of absolution.

True Identity

Let me go further. Often our identity is tied to our view of self. That view may be physical, it may be intellectual, it may be based on age. When trauma occurs, our view of self may be damaged. It could be said, "I was this (immortal, invincible, indestructible, young, etc...), then this event happened and now I am longer what I was. Who am I now?" Any disruption to our view of self changes the normal to something else. Sometimes the desire is to go backward in time to "what was". We can never go back. And therein lies the problem. We yearn for what was lost, and we grieve, however improperly, disjointedly, and incomplete the process. This grief has to be dealt with, so we can move forward.

The question then becomes, "What is the new normal, and what is my place in the new normal?" Another related question has to with unsafe environments, which we will discuss in Chapter 19 under "safe places". These adjustments can be fraught with problems, anxieties, and outright fears. Moving forward is scary. Change is scary. It is scary precisely because it is unknown and unfamiliar. Yes, the unfamiliar is scary, but it may be safer.

The focus of PTSD is rightly on stress, but is often rooted in this search for identity and normality. The answer lies beyond the self. My identity is subsumed in my faith in God through Christ: I am made in the very Image of God (Genesis 1:27). When I realized that God has (and continues to have) plans for me, then I realized that I no longer had to worry about the future. In short then: Who I am resides in Whose I am, and What I do is merely a result.

A key to identity in Christ is found in Acts 17:28, "for in Him we live and move and exist…." If I can find my identity in Christ, I can rise above the past and my pain, and focus on the future.

Because we have a God-who-walks-alongside, the God of hope and healing, we can face and lead others to face trauma head-on, both the effects and the causes. Suffering can be a form of communion with God and identity with Christ. The theology of Christian resurrection, amid unmentionable and indescribable trauma, offers hope. This hope exists, even while facing the devastation that has been evidenced, which often includes death. The future does not remain bleak; the future is something to be strived for. If PTSD causes one to look to the past and see the future as more of the past, then faith enables one to look to the future with hope.

I have found that individuals that do not see themselves as God sees them tend to have more stress. Sometimes we have a script that plays remotely in our brains. It is often learned early and sometimes reinforced by our actions. It is often given to us involuntarily, but we accept it. It can be labels: Worthless, Stupid, Drunk, No-Good, etc. Once we accept the label, it is difficult to remove. I have found that the labels are often untruths, focusing on perhaps one incident. We are not our labels, we are not our past, we are not our failures. I was amazed by how many people thought negatively of themselves, and also thought that God saw them the same way. The only way to combat these labels, these lies of Satan, is to overwrite them with the Truth of God.

Here are some verses I share when this identity of how God see us is broken:

1. Genesis 1:27, "God created man in His own image, in the image of God He created him; male and female He created them." We are made in the Imago Dei, the very image of God.

2. Psalm 139:13-14, "For You formed my inward parts; You wove me in my mother's womb. [14] I will give thanks to You, for I am fearfully and wonderfully made; Wonderful are Your works, And my soul knows it very well." We are made as a supreme work of art, an Opus Magnus, by a Master Craftsman.

3. Jeremiah 1:5a, "Before I formed you in the womb I knew you, And before you were born I consecrated you." Before we were born, God knew us.

4. Isaiah 49:1b, "The LORD called Me from the womb; From the body of my mother He named Me." Before we were born, God chose our name, specifically ours.

5. Jeremiah 29:11, "For I know the plans that I have for you,' declares the LORD, 'plans for welfare and not for calamity to give you a future and a hope."

This is what I then ask of my participants. I give them a new script, what I call "How God Sees Me", to recite to themselves in the mirror everyday:

You are loved by God. You have worth, value,
meaning, and purpose. Nothing you do, or fail
to do, will ever change that. You are a prince
of the Most High, a warrior of God. You are
loved by God.

Be warned: this takes time. It took a long time to believe
a false identity. It also takes a long time to believe in the real
identity, found in the words of God in the Word of God, the
Bible. This is our real identity. If this sounds familiar, if this is
you, then here is your assignment: Recite this new script every
day! Recite them until you believe them. Recite them until you
live them.

Take Aways

If PTSD causes one to look to the past and see the future
as more of the past, then faith enables one to look to the future
with hope. How we see ourselves has a large part in how we
perceive the past and the future. Can we see ourselves as God
sees us? Is there a script playing in our head that is negative?
This script is a lie of Satan. We are not our labels, we are not
our past, we are not our failures. If our past defines us, our
past confines us. We can overwrite that script of lies with a
new script, the Truth of God. Homework: recite this new script,
"How God Sees Me" every day in the mirror until it takes root
in the heart and the mind.

Chapter 8

SOUL INJURY

Soul Injury

W hile we briefly defined this term, as well as "moral injury" and "spiritual injury" in Chapter 2: Operational Definitions, I now want to take the time to discuss them in more detail.

A VA pamphlet reminds us, "Additionally, in certain types of traumatic events, such as war, an individual can be both victim and perpetrator of trauma."[86] Alan Fontana tells us, "Feelings of personal responsibility for killing others and for failing to prevent the death of others are two sets of traumatic experiences that often accompany combat exposure."[87] The APA in their DSM-5 acknowledges this as a peri-traumatic factor that adds a layer to PTSD, "…for military personnel, being a perpetrator, witnessing atrocities, or killing the enemy."[88] Dave

---

[86] "Spirituality and Trauma: Professionals Working Together," 2.

[87] Alan Fontana, and Robert Rosenheck, "Trauma, Change in Strength of Religious Faith, and Mental Health Service Use Among Veterans Treated for PTSD," *The Journal of Nervous and Mental Disease*, 9, Volume 192, (September 2004): 582.

[88] American Psychiatric Association, *DSM-5*, 278.

Grossman reports, "Killing comes with a price, and societies must learn that their soldiers will have to spend the rest of their lives living with what they have done."[89] Kevin Sites, an embedded reporter, quotes one Veteran, "'… it's not what I did in the war, it's what the war did to me.'"[90]

Combat-related PTSD gives rise to many questions, sometimes of an existential nature. Alan Fontana raises this issue, "Similarly, existential questions are qualitatively different from questions of interpersonal and social dysfunction in that the resolution of existential questions requires examination of the bases for moral judgments."[91] This brings up the issues of morals and moral injury. Brett Litz explains morals, "Morals are defined as the personal and shared familial, societal, and legal rules for social behavior, either tacit or explicit. Morals are fundamental assumptions about how things should work and how one should behave in the world."[92] Litz continues, "…moral injury involves an act of transgression that creates dissonance and conflict because it violates assumptions and beliefs about right and wrong and personal goodness."[93] Everett Worthington adds, "Moral injury frequently involves religious

---

[89] Dave Grossman, *On Killing: The Psychological Cost of Learning to Kill in War and Society*. (NY: Back Bay Books, 2009), 194.

[90] Kevin Sites, *The Things They Cannot Say: Stories Soldiers Won't Tell You about What They've Seen, Done or Failed to Do in War*. (NY: Harper Collins Publishers, 2013), 162.

[91] Alan Fontana, 583.

[92] Brett T. Litz, et al., "Moral Injury and Moral Repair in War Veterans: A Preliminary Model and Intervention Strategy," *Clinical Psychology Review*, 2009, 29, 699.

[93] Ibid., 698.

or spiritual conflict."[94] I would also use this definition for spiritual or soul injury.

Presently, moral injury is not considered separate from PTSD. But there are some who feel that PTSD and moral injury are separate and distinct. Rita Nakashima Brock says, "Moral injury is not PTSD."[95] She continues, "Veterans with moral injury have souls in anguish, not a psychological disorder."[96] Brock sees this anguish as theological, not psychological. Therefore, recovery from this type of pain should be spiritual, not psychological.

For others, there seems to be a connection. Shira Maguen explains, "Thus, the key precondition for moral injury is an act of transgression...."[97] A formula could be: **PTSD + transgression = moral injury**. It is not PTSD that leads to moral injury, but PTSD plus an act of transgression. These acts may be more common when PTSD is a result of combat. Within that formula, Litz reports, "Killing, regardless of role, is a better predictor of chronic PTSD symptoms than other indices of combat,

---

[94] Everett L. Worthington and Diane Langberg, "Religious Considerations and Self-Forgiveness in Treating Complex Trauma and Moral Injury in Present and Former Soldiers," *Journal of Psychology and Theology*, 4, Vol 40, (2012): 281.

[95] Rita Nakashima Brock and Gabriella Lettini, *Soul Repair: Recovering from Moral Injury after War*. (Boston: Beacon Press, 2012), xiii.

[96] Ibid., 51.

[97] Shira Maguen and Brett Litz, "Moral Injury in the Context of War," Department of Veterans Affairs, National Center for PTSD. Washington, D.C.: Government Printing Office. http://www.ptsd.va.gov/professional/pages/moral_injury_at_war.asp, 1,(Accessed January 25, 2013.)

mirroring some of the results of atrocities."[98] Worthington echoes that sentiment but adds that killing in combat is "… better than virtually all other indices of combat."[99] And yet, killing, in and of itself, is not a universal guarantee of the onset of PTSD.

Shira Maguen summarizes this by saying, "Transgression is not necessary for a PTSD diagnosis nor does the PTSD syndrome sufficiently capture moral injury (shame, self- handicapping guilt, etc.)"[100] This is information that a pastoral response would need to know. While not all PTSD involves combat, when it constitutes part of the sufferer's PTSD, then a different set of questions need to be asked. While not all PTSD involves a spiritual injury, when the combat PTSD involves acts of transgression, then spiritual injury may be present. There may be a question whether one can have a spiritual injury without any PTSD. It seems logical that spiritual injury would be traumatic and affect the individual deeply.

Both of these terms, "moral injury" and "spiritual injury", may not fully and accurately reflect the pain the sufferer feels. Part of the reason for this may be that not all acts are transgressions but yet may still be causes. An example is driving a car in a neighborhood, obeying all the laws, yet unable to stop in time when a child runs from behind a line of parked cars to chase after a ball. While there may have been no ill intent, still the result is a child is dead. Did the driver transgress a legal or a spiritual law? No. Did the driver cause the child's death? Yes.

---

[98] Brett Litz, 697.

[99] Everett L. Worthington, 278.

[100] Shira Maguen, 2.

Another concern is not the denotation, but the connotation of either moral injury or spiritual injury. Frankly, there is baggage with both terms. The most common concern I have heard with spiritual injury is, "I'm not spiritual." And with moral injury, does the term go deep enough? Is there something deeper than violating one's moral center?

Consider the term "soul injury" that Deborah Grassman defines as "the un-mourned grief and unforgiven guilt that sometimes lingers in war's aftermath."[101] My definition differs somewhat in that *soul injury is trauma that wounds our soul, which affects our connection to God, which affects our connection to one another.* Utilizing both these definitions, we highlight both the grief and the guilt so the term "soul injury" combines the best of what we are trying to say when we use the terms "moral injury" or "spiritual injury" interchangeably. It further emphasizes a causal factor without emphasizing a transgression. The formula then becomes: **combat PTSD = soul injury + PTSD**. This is the operating definition we will use.

Age as a Filter

Even within this framework, why do two people, who have gone through similar events experience them differently? An example is Eli Wiesel and Victor Frankl. Both were Jews that experienced the horror of concentration camps during the Nazi Holocaust in WWII. Both lost family members, experienced privation, saw untold horrors. And yet, these experiences did

---

[101] Deborah Grassman, "Wounded Warriors: Their Last Battle," Conference presentation, Midland, TX, March 6, 2015.

not break the spirit of Frankl, who said "man can preserve a vestige of spiritual freedom, of independence of mind, even in such terrible conditions of psychic and physical stress."[102] Frankl wrote of his experiences in the concentration camps, as stated previously, "If there is meaning in life at all, then there must be meaning in suffering."[103] Contrast this with Wiesel, who spoke about his experiences, "Never shall I forget those moments which murdered my God and my soul and turned my dreams to dust."[104]

Dohrenwend, et al, may have the answer to that question: prior traumatic experiences, prior mental health issues, and age.[105] Why age? This relates to the spiritual core of who humans are, and how present experiences are filtered or seen through the lenses of past experiences. In other words, age may add to one's moral filter, giving it the ability necessary to filter out what harms one. Without age, without some expo-sure to the world through experience, one's moral filters may easily be overwhelmed. Consider that Frankl, at age 37, was an established psychiatrist before he was sent to the concen-tration camp at Auschwitz; before he was sent to Auschwitz, Wiesel was a teenager.

It is interesting to note an older Wiesel was asked the question, "Do you still have faith in God as the ultimate redeemer?" His response may show the use of age as a filter, not just prior to a traumatic experience, but even after the

---

[102] Victor E. Frankl, 65.

[103] Ibid., 67.

[104] Eli Wiesel, *Night*. (NY: Bantam Books, 1982), 32.

[105] Bruce Dohrenwend, 14-15.

traumatic experiences, I would be within my rights to give up faith in God, and I could invoke six million reasons to justify such a decision. But I am incapable of straying from the path charted by my forefathers, who felt duty-bound to live for God. Without the faith of my ancestors, my own faith in humanity would be diminished. So my wounded faith endures.[106]

It seems as if Wiesel was able to reframe his experiences through the lens of age and accumulated experiences, including the processing of his religious faith. Neither age nor time negates the experiences; rather, it reframes them in light of other experiences. The past is brought into the present, and filtered, for use in the future. Perhaps this reframing is a continual exercise and is necessary.

There are some that say the past is too painful to revisit. But if someone is stuck in the past, stuck in the pain, stuck in the trauma, stuck in the event, then that visit is an everyday overwhelming thing. Our past then becomes a dark, dank, jail, not letting the light of a new day shine its warmth, love, and peace. We need to revisit that event, bring it forward to the present, and integrate it into our future. Our past can inform our future without over-whelming it.

As we revisit our past, we can train ourselves to see it in different light. Know that the past does not change; the only thing that does change is our perspective. How do I reframe the past? The filter of age is a useful tool. Age means knowing oneself better, acquiring hard-won tools with which to weigh

---

[106] Aron Hirt-Manheimer, "Against Indifference: A Conversation with Elie Wiesel," *Reform Judaism Online*. http://reformjudaismmag.org/Articles/index.cfm?id=1074&goback=%2Egde_108049_member_5909686850427043843,(Accessed August 26, 2014.)

the world, knowing what issues (imaginary or real) tend to suck our time and peace, and which issues need our attention. I choose which things those are. We choose what things occupy our mind.

Sometimes, we can replace a thought with another thought. Do I look at the glass as half-full or half-empty? How and why do I reach that decision? It often has to do with experience, which is almost always personal, i.e., my experience. Are there other experiences that are not mine? Yes. There are empirical experiences, recorded experiences of others. We can experience pirates in a Robert Louis Stevenson novel, know about inventions such as the light bulb or the telephone, almost taste the salt of the ocean in an Ernest Hemingway novel, or feel the winter cold in a Robert Frost poem. We can experience them through the author's eyes, using his words to paint a picture where we can feel, where we can vicariously experience.

The same holds true for the Bible. I can read about the Apostle Paul, then read his own words recording his experiences, and learn from them, without having to repeat them. I can see the Truth come alive in the pages even if I had never thought of that before. My view of the world changes as I learn. And I change as well.

Take Aways

Soul injury is trauma that wounds our soul, which affects our connection to God, which affects our connection to one another. How we interpret events in our lives may be due to many factors: prior traumatic experiences, prior mental health issues, and age. Neither age nor time negates the experiences;

rather, it reframes them in light of other experiences, including the processing of his religious faith. The past is brought into the present, and filtered, for use in the future. Perhaps this reframing is a continual exercise and is necessary. Ultimately, we choose what things occupy our mind.

Chapter 9

FORGIVENESS

Forgiveness

In Matthew 9:2-8, we read,

> And they brought to Him a paralytic lying on a bed. Seeing their faith, Jesus said to the paralytic, "Take courage, son; your sins are forgiven." [3] And some of the scribes said to themselves, "This *fellow* blasphemes." [4] And Jesus knowing their thoughts said, "Why are you thinking evil in your hearts? [5] Which is easier, to say, 'Your sins are forgiven,' or to say, 'Get up, and walk'? [6] But so that you may know that the Son of Man has authority on earth to forgive sins"—then He said to the paralytic, "Get up, pick up your bed and go home." [7] And he got up and went home. [8] But when the crowds saw *this*, they were awestruck, and glorified God, who had given such authority to men.

This passage underscores forgiveness, or rather how we often see forgiveness. The Jewish scribes said that Jesus blasphemed, i.e., took God's name in vain. Why did they believe this? Because they rightly ascertained that only God can forgive, and since only God can forgive, then forgiveness is a miracle. They thought that ascribing that miracle to mere humans would minimize the miraculous wonder of forgiveness. In one way they are correct. Do we trivialize forgiveness to the extent it has no power? Do we, in effect, say, "Pass the potatoes, I forgive you, pass the salt?" Do we somehow forget or not recognize that the power of forgiveness is a miracle? Contrasting this view of forgiveness as common, we do seem to recognize that healing is a miracle. We often pray for healing. The Jews in this passage agreed. They thought healing was a miracle. They did not get angry that Jesus performed miracles of healing, except when it was on the wrong day, the Sabbath. They did get angry that He ascribed the miracle of forgiveness to Himself. Do we often reverse this, and accept healing as a miracle, but not forgiveness? We tend to downplay that Jesus gave us this miraculous power of forgiveness to forgive others. We need to be in continual awe, like the crowds mentioned in v.8, "But when the crowds saw this, they were awestruck, and glorified God, who had given such authority to men."

We also tend to minimize the power and completeness of God's forgiveness. Hebrews 8:12 tells us, "For I will be merciful to their iniquities, and I will remember their sins no more." God chooses to not remember our sins once we repent of them, asking for His forgiveness.

The Bible describes the unfathomability of God's forgiveness in Psalm 103:11-12,

> For as high as the heavens are above the earth,
> So great is His lovingkindness toward those
> who fear Him.
>
> As far as the east is from the west, So far has He
> removed our transgressions from us.

Both of these passages taken together tell us that God will forgive us our sins, not hold it against us, and choose to not remember. This is a promise of God.

To be clear, psychology encourages forgiveness, mainly because it helps the individual move on. Theology agrees but also explains why: 1) If we do not forgive others, then God will not forgive us. (Matthew 6:15) 2) If God lives in us, we want to do what is right, out of love for God and for others. (Acts 10:35, I John 4:19)

Self-Forgiveness

The reintegration of self may require exploring the concept of forgiveness, especially that of self-forgiveness. Forgiving oneself may be the hardest area of forgiveness to achieve, and perhaps even to seek. Julie Hall points out, "…reconciliation with the self is necessary in self-forgiveness."[107] What this means is that, "In order to truly forgive oneself, one must either explicitly or implicitly acknowledge that one's behavior was wrong and accept the responsibility of blame for such

---

[107] Julie H. Hall and Frank D. Fingham, "Self-Forgiveness: The Stepchild of Forgiveness Research," *Journal of Social and Clinical Psychology*, 5, Vol 24, (2005): 624.

behavior."[108] The question for some Veterans is, interestingly, not if God will forgive them, but if they will forgive themselves. As referenced at the beginning of this book, one Veteran I interviewed, Veteran B, put it this way, "Even if God could forgive me, I can't forgive myself." Litz informs us, "The more time passes, the more service members will be convinced that not only their actions, but they are unforgiveable. In other words, service members and Veterans with moral injury will fail to see a path toward renewal and reconciliation; they will fail to forgive themselves and experience self-condemnation."[109] This self-condemnation can be manifested with such behaviors as "...shame, guilt, demoralization, self-handicapping behaviors (e.g., self-sabotaging relationships), and self-harm (e.g., para-suicidal behaviors)."[110] This may happen when forgiving oneself is seen as a sign of disrespect, as Hall points out, "A second frequent concern related to self-forgiveness is that it is a sign of disrespect toward the victim, and thus is only appropriate after the offender is granted forgiveness by the victim."[111] This does bring up the question: if the victim dies, does this death negate the possibility of being forgiven and forgiving the self? Hall seems to answer this: "When an offender acknowledges and accepts responsibility for wrongdoing and is willing to apologize or make restitution to the victim, self-forgiveness is not a sign of disrespect."[112] This may be an intention if not an action. Finally, it is seen as a good sign that God can forgive, "There

---

[108] Ibid., 626

[109] Brett T. Litz, 700.

[110] Shira Maguen, 1.

[111] Julie H. Hall, 628.

[112] Ibid. 628.

is preliminary evidence to suggest that perceived forgiveness from God is positively associated with self-forgiveness."[113] We will look more at this when we discuss accepting God's forgiveness. Worthington adds, "Often self-condemnation drives people to recognize their wrongdoing and further drives them back to God seeking forgiveness, healing, and restoration."[114]

Going back to moral injury, Worthington links the two, "Self-forgiveness is the culmination of moral repair (initiated by God's conviction and fulfilled by God's mercy and Jesus' sacrificial love), and the derivative social repair and psychological repair."[115] Worthington has designed an alliterative acrostic for steps to responsible self- forgiveness that anyone dealing with sufferers of PTSD could embrace, but especially pastoral counselors.[116]

There are six steps:

Step 1: Receive God's forgiveness

Step 2: Repair relationships

Step 3: Rethink ruminations

Step 4: REACH emotional self-forgiveness

R= recall hurt without blame
E= emotional replacement

---

[113] Ibid., 630.

[114] Everett L. Worthington, 277.

[115] Ibid., 282.

[116] Ibid., 284-285.

A= altruistic gift of forgiveness
C= committing publicly to forgiveness experienced
H= holding on to forgiveness when doubts arise

Step 5: Rebuild self-acceptance

Step 6: Resolve to live virtuously

This last step of Worthington: Resolving to live virtuously, is akin to the concept of spiritual growth. What is meant by spiritual growth? It is a maturation of faith, a deeper level of faith. Confession highlights a conversation sufferers have with themselves, as well as with others and with God. For some, to confess means not to deny anymore. Only in the admission can there be growth.

Forgiving God

Julie Exline has brought up another concern in the realm of forgiveness: forgiving God. She says, "What exactly does it mean to forgive God? Even if people do not believe that God has willfully harmed them, they may become intensely angry if they believe that God caused or allowed some highly painful or unfair event to occur."[117] As God can do no wrong, then forgiving God is a theological impossibility, but it may still be a practical reality. While some may struggle with this concept, this inability to forgive God impacts the faith of many of the Veterans I see. Exline continues, "Such perceptions

---

[117] Julie J. Exline, Ann M. Yali, and Marci Lobel, "When God Disappoints: Difficulty Forgiving God and its Role in Negative Emotion," *Journal of Health Psychology*, 3, Vol 4, Issue 3, (1999): 366.

may prompt intense feelings of betrayal and rage, especially if God's actions are perceived as intentional, unjustifiable, and highly damaging."[118]

This theological question: "Did God allow or did God cause this event, this suffering?" is not an easy question to answer. Not to sidestep, but often when this question is asked of me, there is another question underneath, "Does God love me?" This may be asked in terms of "What did I do wrong?", "Why is God is punishing me?", "Does God still have plans for me?", and "Is God loving?" All of these questions are questions of worth, value, meaning, and purpose. I ask them to elaborate, "What do you mean when you ask this?" If I find that the question is one of the ones listed above, I can then respond to their pain. To the question of "Does God love me?" I respond with a resounding "Yes!" Only after finding the root question are we able to address other questions. I do add that God is grieving with them, a sharing of pain. To answer their question without knowing the journey they have crossed is to not help them. It really does help to ask questions of them to find their real question. Sometimes they do not know the question they are really asking, the one they want answers to. My role is to walk with them, often on their journey of self- discovery.

A VA pamphlet[119] favors asking about a patient's beliefs, using these questions that may be asked by anybody, as a spirituality tool:

These questions are likely a useful starting place....

---

[118] Ibid., 367.

[119] Ibid., 3.

1. Are you affiliated with a religious or spiritual community?

2. Do you see yourself as a religious or spiritual person? If so, in what way?

3. Has the event affected your religiousness and if so, in what ways?

4. Has your religion or spirituality been involved in the way you have coped with this event? If so, in what way?

Confession also involves the sufferer's participation, his/her choosing a direction. Smith notes, "So, confession is often the beginning of a new sense of the weight and meaninglessness of our acts, and the need to choose, to commit ourselves and shapes our lives purposefully and consistently."[120] AA maintains that confession is necessary for recovery from SUD; so, too for PTSD.

Accepting Forgiveness

When one Vietnam Vet said, "Even if God could forgive me, I can't forgive myself," I heard, "My God is not big enough." We worked on his view of God, as well as his view of forgiveness. If you can put God in a box, then your view of God is too small. Let Him out of that human box! God is simply too large, too grand, too awesome, too mysterious, and way beyond our

---

[120] Martin L. Smith, 44.

understanding to be put in a box! Even if I had the sum of the world's knowledge, experience, creativity, logic, and intelligence, I am still a finite being. Can a finite being fully comprehend an infinite God? No, that would be illogical. When we think that faith in God is illogical, we try to limit God to human logic. When God acts in ways that do not conform to our logic, perhaps it is because there is a logic we both do not nor cannot understand, a supra-logic, a logic beyond ourselves. God, as the Supreme Being, acts according to his own supra-logic, His Supreme Logic.

Many Veterans have a problem with forgiveness on all levels, but particularly of self. Why? I have met many Veterans who do not like themselves, are ashamed of who they have become, and cannot find a way out of that, so they often use alcohol and/or drugs to help them forget or not remember, at least temporarily. The method and the effect of this solution (substance abuse) is always temporary. And reality always comes after. Make no mistake: self-forgiveness is hard work. Working through the 12 Steps of AA helps one take an honest appraisal of oneself, finding which areas need improvement, which helps bring forgiveness. People undertake the 12 Steps because they want to be sober, but also because they want to be a different person, to live honestly and not lie to themselves, and ultimately, to forgive and like themselves, and the program helps achieve that.

Forgetting

War has a way of uniting or dividing people. Sometimes the enemy we fight is not the one our country is against. Sometimes it is our own nature, sometimes it is that of others.

My confession: I hated someone with every fiber of my being. Hate is a destructive feeling … and I knew that. After my wartime experiences as an officer of Marines, I came home, resigned my commission, went to seminary, accepted a commission in the Navy, and came on active duty as a Navy chaplain, often to Marines. It had been several years since I had seen or even thought about this person. In fact, I had forgotten about him. *I had not forgiven him, I had just forgotten about him.* People often say, "I may forgive him, but I will never forget about what he has done to me." For me it was, "I may forget about him, but I will never forgive him." Both of these sayings come from the same source: a hard heart. Both lead to the same place: Hell. Matthew 6:14-15, "For if you forgive others for their transgressions, your heavenly Father will also forgive you. But if you do not forgive others, then your Father will not forgive your transgressions." If I do not forgive, how can I be forgiven? If God has forgiven me of so much, how can I not forgive someone of so little? If I claim to want to follow Christ, but do not forgive, how can I have a relationship with Him? How can I have a right relationship based on honesty? Have I made what Step 4 of AA calls, "a searching and fearless moral inventory of myself?"

Back to my story: on one of my first assignments as a new Navy chaplain, I saw the object of my hate. When I saw him, all those feelings I had stuffed away came roaring back, as fresh as it was yesterday. Like a dog burying a bone that he digs up a few days later, it stunk and will continue to stink! I hated him anew, but now the hate was mixed with shame and guilt for doing so. I rationalized that hate was okay as a Marine, but that reasoning did not flow well as a chaplain. God knew I had to model forgiveness if I was going to preach it. I could not truly forget until I had truly forgiven. Sometimes God seems to have a really odd sense of humor.

Forgiveness of Others

Let me explain what forgiveness is not:

1. It is not condoning the actions of another or even of myself. My friend's daughter was killed during a robbery. Initially my friend was paralyzed with anger and plans of retribution, until God "got ahold" of him and taught him love, which manifested in forgiveness. He tried to witness to the culprits, now inmates, but they would not listen to love. Even though forgiven, they are still guilty of taking a human life.

2. It is not removing the natural effect of the sin. If someone robs a bank, the teller may forgive the person, but the police and judicial system will have their day in court. This is a natural consequence of our behavior.

3. It is not allowing sin to remain in effect. If someone hurts my child, I may forgive them, but I will put safeguards in place so that does not happen again.

4. It is not trivializing the action or pain. If there is a rape before forgiveness, there is still a rape after. We still have to deal with the ravages of the action and the effects of the pain.

I realized that I had to forgive, but I could not. How can we forgive someone who has wronged us deeply? *We can if we but let God do so.* I had to let God soften my heart so I could forgive. I had to pray to God to help me forgive, or even, to give me the heart and the capacity to forgive when it was beyond my human capacity. And God did. When I let God help me forgive, a feeling of peace came over me.

Some may ask, "What if the person doesn't think he needs to be forgiven? What if he never repents?" These are valid questions. In my case, the object of my hate, then the object of my forgiveness, did not repent. That is between him and God, and between them only. But between God and me, there is now no block. If I had not forgiven him, I would have given him power to be a wedge between us, blocking Heavenly blessings. Forgiveness removed that power, restoring the path of blessings.

We have discussed what forgiveness is, is not, and how it is necessary to forgive. We also discussed how easy it is to do: let God do the heavy lifting, to mold our will into His, to let us see others through His eyes, to love. It is easy, yet often it is also the hardest thing I have done. Easy but difficult. Easy but hard to do, mainly because we get in the way.

Sometimes, for many different reasons, it is not healthy to try to find the person who has wronged you. The same holds true when someone dies who has wronged you. Especially with the latter, you will never get the satisfaction of hearing their true remorse or regret. Do not let that stop you from forgiveness. If you give that person power to stop the flow of blessings, then you can remove that same power through forgiveness. One method that can be helpful to you when forgiving someone may be difficult is the concept of the "Empty Chair". Imagine the object of the forgiveness impasse sitting across from you, then carry out a conversation with them. Conversation, not mono-logue. Since there are always at least two parties to a wrong, then ask the invisible person seated across from you for for-giveness, then take the opportunity to forgive them as well. You have now removed whatever power they had over you, and are released to Peace and Joy.

Take Aways

Forgiveness has many parts: forgiveness, self-forgiveness, forgiving God, accepting forgiveness, forgetting/not forgetting, and forgiveness of others. It is hard, but possible, if we can let God help us. The concept of the "Empty Chair" may help when we are stuck.

Chapter 10

GRIEF

Grief

In discussing PTSD we need to discuss grief. We grieve when we lose something. The more the importance, the deeper we grieve. This is natural. What is unnatural is not addressing the grief. Grief, unaddressed, can attract more grief, adding layers, becoming complex grief. Complex grief takes time to unravel.

In 1969, Elisabeth Kübler-Ross wrote a ground-breaking book, *On Death and Dying*, in which she listed at least five stages of grief. She did this after observing cancer victims, specifically female cancer victims. Many people embrace this book as a guide to dealing with death, especially the terminally ill. Some use it to recognize stages they have been in, perhaps stuck in. There are others who question whether the stages transfer across issues like gender and non-cancer deaths. In my own work, her work has been helpful, but only in the sense I had a larger toolbox that I could sample from. Because people often quote this book, I have listed it in the Works Consulted.

My goal in dealing with grief is to be Present. My presence is calm, non-judgmental, and caring. We each need to be aware of how we react to our own emotions. Sometimes I need a poker face. Faced with a story that goes beyond my experience or even my imagination, I cannot let on that the story may bother me. Other times, the emotion I feel lets me connect to the one in pain. I have listened to many types of stories, including stories of grieving a past loss or the grief of a loss happening presently.

We often communicate by speaking. But use of our vocal chords is only a small percentage of our total communication process. We often use non-verbal cues such as body language, posture, or facial gestures. There are many other ways to communicate, especially when we are dealing with pain. Here is a list I use when words do not suffice, what I have termed, "When Words Won't Work":

1. *The Eloquence of Silence.* In Job 2:13 we find this amazing passage, "Then they sat down on the ground with him for seven days and seven nights with no one speaking a word to him, for they saw that *his* pain was very great." Silence seems painful. Sometimes we fill the air with words so we don't feel awkward. To listen in silence is often an eloquent communication.

2. *The Communion of Tears.* I admit there are times, many times, that when I hear a story that I start to cry. I am not ashamed, for that emotion often lets me connect with another person's pain. Tears speak a language that words can only approximate. And tears are cathartic, washing away toxins from both our bodies and our souls.

3. *The Power of Touch*. Touch connects us as humans. A touch on the arm or a side hug conveys a warm humanity, a feeling that we are not alone in this world.

Recently, I had vocal chord surgery and could not speak for a time. I "spoke" by writing, texting, pantomiming, or sometimes using ASL (American Sign Language), of which I know just a few phrases or words. My pantomimes, I must admit, were not often "spot on", and were sometimes hilarious. I soon discovered it was sometimes too difficult to attempt to convey my thoughts. It took a lot of time. I was frustrated, often because it took a lot of time, and necessitated both focused attention and intentionality. Going further, I discovered that not all of my thoughts needed to be expressed. I used the silence to weigh what I really wanted to convey. Was it worth the trouble? Did it need to be said? Choosing what needed to be said, or not said, made me appreciate the silence. This affected me so much that when I could speak, I chose to speak sparingly.

Each individual is different. Each person's response to trauma is different. Our response to trauma is based on many factors, among them: life experience, previous trauma, age, faith, family, and support systems that include individuals and groups. And the type of grief to trauma is also affected by the type of loss.

Loss of Life

We grieve the loss of life. We are impacted if we see the death, more impacted if we know the dead, even more impacted if we somehow caused the death. How close we are to the death and the dead determine the level of grief.

PTSD can be an event, or a series of events. PTSD involving death can be a one-time event of a single death, a one-time event of multiple deaths, or it can be over several events. It can happen over time, perhaps even years. All of these details can build layers of grief, where each layer needs to be addressed.

The most natural therapy, yet often the most difficult, is to talk about those experiences. This is when safe places are needed. This is where faith, family, and friends have an impact. This is when we listen, without bias or prejudice, but with our hearts. This also when we hear about guilt, shame, and unforgiveness. The "if I could have/would have/should have" mantra is often used. This is a detrimental thought that leads nowhere because the reality doesn't change no matter how much we wish it to. The chapters on Forgiveness, on Soul Injury, and on Listening may help.

Loss of Identity

PTSD is not just about death. There are many types of loss. It can be something physical. I saw a lot of Veterans at the VA who were missing limbs. They grieved their loss. The rehabilitation process could be lengthy, painful, and frustrating. Prosthetics are not just about strapping on a new leg. It is taking what used to be an almost automatic function without thought but now requires a high degree of concentration and intentionality. When I received new knees from the VA, I would spend time looking at them, willing them to do what I wanted them to do, because the previous pathways were altered. It is no surprise that for some disabled Veterans, their self-image suffers to the point where they see themselves as, using their own words: "incomplete", "a half-man", or "less than a man". The perception does not have to mirror reality; rather, the perception is the reality they live in. The chapters on Guilt/Shame, on Forgiveness, and on Imago Dei speak to this troubling mindset.

Sometimes the loss is not physical, or not just physical. Sometimes the loss is purely a loss of self-image or identity. Grieving the loss of identity or self-image, as discussed previously, can alter reality. We can see the sufferer one way, while they see themselves in a completely different manner. Again, we have to be aware of their perception of reality before they can see or we can help them see beyond the perception, or misperception, to what is real.

One example shows that self-image does not have to be based on reality. When we are young we often see ourselves as invincible and immortal, because our history has proved that and sometimes our training emphasizes it. Veteran S, a Marine, said this about his self-image,

I was a young Corporal with one deployment under my belt. Yes sir-eee I was ten foot tall and bullet proof. Still fully indoctrinated in invincibility still full of pride and rage. I thought that all men should fear me, and that all woman wanted to bed me.

Another sufferer, a burn victim, spoke about the incident where he got burned, the painful debridement process, the process of rehabilitation, his retraining for a different career, and his many successes since. His comment shocked me, "I wish they had let me die." This was long after the burn incident, long after the recovery. This speaks to both pain and to self-image. Which speaks louder? Somewhere there is a disconnect. But between what, exactly? Perhaps it is between how he sees himself and how God sees him, which we discussed in Chapter 18: Imago Dei.

Certain trauma makes a mockery of youthful self-images of invincibility, immortality, and of the concept that this present moment will never change. When we lose our self-image, the loss is devastating. Whether a loss of life or a loss of self-image, these all affect our image of self.

Conversely, how I see myself, my identity, affects how I grieve. If my perception of self is clouded, then restoration of that self has to wait until that self is identified. I cannot help myself until I know who I am.

Take Aways

We grieve when we suffer a loss. The loss may be a death. When communicating to those who are grieving a death, words sometimes do not suffice. This is when we can use the "When Words Won't Work" matrix: the Eloquence of Silence, the Communion of Tears, and the Power of Touch to communicate heart to heart. Loss can also be something physical like the loss of a limb. Sometimes it is a loss of identity or self-image. Our perception of self becomes reality, even if the perception is a misperception of reality. We need to be aware of perceptions, especially our own. How we see ourselves affects how we grieve.

Chapter 11

PRAYER

Prayer

I n formatting a pastoral theology of care for Veterans with
PTSD, there is at least one principle that must be addressed,
remembered, and kept foremost in the mind. Mark Gignilliat,
in exploring Karl Barth in his *Church Dogmatics*, says, "For
Barth, all of one's theological exegetical labours from beginning to end must take place in the context of prayer."[121] He continues, "It conceives of the entire exegetical task as first and
foremost an obedient exercise of prayer."[122] This principle of
prayer before exegesis[123], of seeing what the text says, has just
as much weight in formulating a pastoral theology of care for
Veterans with PTSD. We are called to bathe the process, as well
as the individual sufferer and the counselor, in prayer.

What kind of prayer? There are many types of prayer, as
evidenced by the many books on the subject in both secular

---

[121] Mark Gignilliat, "Ora et Labora: Barth's Forgotten Hermeneutical
Principle," *Expository Times*, 6, Vol 120, (March 2009): 277.

[122] Ibid., 280.

[123] Exegesis is simply letting the text speak, as opposed to isogesis, which
is reading into the text what one wants it to say. The text here is the Bible.

and Christian bookstores. A quick perusal shows titles like, *The ACTS Prayer, The Prayer of Jabez, Daniel's Prayer,* and *The Lord's Prayer*. While each of these prayers have a focus and application, the specific type of prayer can be left up to the individual. I am more interested in discussing the purpose, the power, and the practice of prayer.

What is the *purpose* of prayer? It is to know the mind of Christ and the will of God. It is to align oneself with that will. It is to change hearts and situations; this often means that the heart of the one who prays is changed. The founder of the Church of Nazarene, Phineas F. Bresee, put it this way, "The aim of the prayer meeting is to get heaven open and the glory down."[124]

We often pray when prayer is all we have. We come in apparent weakness, but leave filled with power. II Corinthians 12:9 says, "And He has said to me, 'My grace is sufficient for you, for power is perfected in weakness.' Most gladly, therefore, I will rather boast about my weaknesses, so that the power of Christ may dwell in me." This type of prayer is passionate: out of our hearts, with our whole being, wrestling with God, as Jacob did at Peniel as recorded in Genesis 32:24-32. When we look at Jacob wrestling with God, and especially not letting go of God, we see the glory of God abiding.

What is the *power* of prayer? Prayer can change both hearts and situations. Remembering James 5:16, "Therefore, confess your sins to one another, and pray for one another so that you may be healed. The effective prayer of a righteous man can accomplish much." How much can be accomplished is evidenced in the Bible itself. In Exodus 32, we see that evidence

---

[124] Cory Jones, "Repairing the Altar in the Church," http://nmi.nazarene. org/workshops/Files/Workshops/106/106JonesRepairingtheAltar2013. pdf, (Accessed April 17, 2015).

in a very real way when God declares to Moses His intention to destroy the Israelites. Moses then intercedes for the people. And in Exodus 32:14 we see this amazing sentence on the effects of that intercession, "So the Lord changed His mind about the harm which He said He would do to His people." See the effect of prayer from one person who prays passionately! God does hear, and listen to, our prayers!

What is the *practice* of prayer? The first part of the passage in James tells us to confess to, and pray for, one another. One can assume this means to do so often. Matthew 6:33 tells us, "But seek first His kingdom and His righteousness." We are to seek God: to seek His will, to seek His face, to seek Him. This is the spiritual discipline of prayer, a practice that I encourage the sufferer to adopt.

I find that once we are ready to pray, I invite the sufferer to tell what he or she wants me to pray for. I then pray for that. I have found that over time, the focus of the prayer changes, from self to others, from inward to outward. If the sufferer has been seeking God, then prayer moves from praying for just things (situations, people), to seeking God's heart and praying to have the heart of God, seeing others as God sees us.

I was in a bunker, hunkering down because enemy SCUD missiles were traveling overhead, destination unknown. Next to us in the port was a cargo ship carrying tons of ammunition of all types, including high-explosive shells. If a SCUD had hit that ammunition ship, the port would have become a crater. As I was in the bunker, I prayed. I knew that my wife and her prayer guild back home in Texas were praying. But, at that moment, I felt her prayers. God allowed me to see that her prayers were working. I knew then that I would come home. I no longer feared I would become a casualty.

This experience combined head knowledge with heart knowledge. Now I can say I know what I believe, but even more importantly, I can say why I know what I believe. There have been many experiences of prayer coming alive in me. Prayer changes things. Colossians 1:13-14 says, "For He rescued us from the domain of darkness, and transferred us to the kingdom of His beloved Son, in whom we have redemption, the forgiveness of sins." A God who can deliver me from darkness to Light, from un-redemption to redemption, from unforgiveness to forgiveness, and from the kingdom of Satan to the kingdom of Christ can change any situation and any person. Sometimes the person changed is the one who prays. Prayer is the vehicle God uses to converse with us, if we but listen. If God listens to the prayer of, and in my heart, then my heart can hear God as well.

Take Aways

Prayer has a purpose. There is power in prayer, with results. If we get into the practice of prayer, our prayer changes from an inward to an outward focus. All of these impact our faith, moving us from knowing "what I know", to knowing "why I know what I know".

Chapter 12

HOPE

Hope

K enneth Graham, on commenting on Storm Swain's research at Ground Zero for 9/11, quotes her:

> A resurrection mentality neither denies nor negates death but, rather, affirms that which is life giving beyond death, a resurrection life where one, at least in the case of Jesus in the Gospels, still bears scars of death but lives with them. This can be as profound as experiencing the presence of God and a transformation of self and as simple as the life-giving things one needs to do to live in the face of a disaster in the midst of a community of care.[125]

---

[125] Larry K. Graham, "Trauma and Transformation at Ground Zero: A Pastoral Theology," *Journal of Pastoral Theology*, 2, Vol 22, (Winter 2012): 7-4.

This theology of Christian resurrection amid unmentionable and indescribable trauma offers hope, while facing the devastation that has been evidenced, which often includes death. Facing trauma head-on, both the effects and the causes, allows recovery efforts to focus on the God-who-walks-alongside, the God of hope and healing.

This concept of God-who-walks-alongside may be attributed to Edward Shillebeeckx, who formulated a theology of suffering. Elizabeth Kennedy Tillar describes his theology in this way,

> His concept of beneficial suffering is defined in a two-fold way: (1) compassionate, inter-subjective service to individuals and (2) a critical orientation to unjust socio-political structures that dehumanize or oppress people. Suffering for others can take several forms, which are not perceived as exclusive of each other: suffering vicariously, instead of others; suffering with others for their benefit; and expiatory self-sacrifice. In Schillebeeckx's theology, suffering in any form is redemptive when it is unmitigated self-surrender through and for others in unwavering communion with God.[126]

---

[126] Elizabeth K. Tillar, "Suffering for Others in the Theology of Edward Schillebeeckx," PhD dissertation, January 1, 2000. ETD Collection for Fordham University. Paper AA19955973. http://fordham.bepress.com/dissertations/AA19955973, 1, (Accessed July 9, 2012.)

Kathleen McManus adds this thought from Schillebeeckx, "... it is only obedience to God that can save us from—or rather through—suffering, sin, and evil."[127] The strength to come through suffering comes from God. She adds that Jesus' connection to humanity "lies in Jesus' own relationship of unbroken communion with God through suffering and death."[128] Suffering can be a form of communion with God and identity with Christ. This expression of suffering for and with others may be a vital link in recovery.

Sometimes hope can be kept alive by what we notice and appreciate. Tick speaks about one thing that may do this, namely beauty, "Beauty offers order, purpose and grace... without beauty your soul dies."[129] Sometimes an appreciation of what is beautiful, and this can be anything, can get us through the suffering.

Hope is vital to recovery, to reconciliation, to transformation. But, can we have hope without faith? Hope believes in the Eternal, and that because we know the Author of Life, then Death is but the passage to Eternity. Suffering can be tolerated as long as there is Hope. Appreciating what is around us, in that moment, helps us to validate suffering.

Take Aways

A theology of suffering may offer hope. This includes the theology of Christian resurrection amid unmentionable

---

[127] Kathleen McManus, "Suffering in the Theology of Edward Schillebeeckx," *Theological Studies* 60, (1999): 486.

[128] Ibid., 480.

[129] Edward Tick, 20.

and indescribable trauma. This is grounded in the God-who-walks-alongside, the God of hope and healing. The strength to come through suffering comes from God.

Chapter 13

PERSONALITY

Personality

In teaching, one learns that students learn differently. Some may be auditory learners, while some are more visual. Some need to hear themselves recite, and others learn kinesthetically, by doing. Just as there are different learning styles, there are different personality styles or attitudes. Isabel Myers and her mother Katherine Briggs, in developing the Myers-Briggs Temperament Inventory (MBTI), differentiated between the "attitudes" of introversion and extraversion. In extraversion, "attention seems to flow out, or to be drawn out, to the objects and people of the environment. There is a desire to act on the environment to affirm its importance, to increase its effect."[130] This is understood to be where one recharges, where one feels ready to face a new day: with and around others. Public settings are desirable.

Conversely, in introversion, "energy is drawn from the environment and consolidated within one's position. The main interests of the introvert are in the inner world of concepts and

---

[130] Isabel Briggs Myers and Mary H. McCaulley, *Manual: A Guide to the Development and Use of the Myers-Briggs Temperament Indicator.* (Palo Alto, CA: Consulting Psychologists Press, 1985), 13.

ideas."[131] This is understood to be that one recharges in solitude and solitary activities. These may be activities as diverse as curling up around a book to read, communing with nature, walking the dogs, and hiking alone. The emphasis is not to be around other people.

The significance of this distinction between introversion and extraversion as personality attitudes is directly related to recovery efforts. How one relates to another may help determine the coping mechanisms that are used to aid in recovery. Where does one get strength to stay clean, dry, and sober? From others? From oneself? Where is the support system? From a group? From a select few individuals?

To know the answers to these questions is to know an aspect of one's personality, and to know oneself helps to identify support systems that are vital in the recovery process. For example, AA has group meetings, which seems to help those with extraversion, but it also supports an individual sponsor, which seems to help those with introversion. Interestingly, AA uses both, without regard to either extraverts or introverts. It has groups that extraverts may find comfortable and familiar, but introverts may find uncomfortable and unfamiliar. It has a one-on-one with a sponsor that may appeal to introverts but may not be appealing to extraverts.

The same can be said for the military, especially chaplains and the chapel. When I was a military chaplain, the chapel was a place of refuge, both stateside and in foreign lands. But, I did not limit myself to the confines of the chapel. I went where my congregation was. In the business world, this is called, "Leadership

---

[131] Ibid., 13.

by Walking Around". Sometimes the best sermon is not the one that uses words.

It is good to know our personality type and preferred method of stress reducing, of coping, and of recharging. But we need to realize that our lives intersect with others, that we are exposed to other personality types, and that we have to operate in a world both like ourselves and unlike ourselves. AA shows that we need to use and interact with both types of personality in order to go forward.

I am an introvert. I do solitary activities to recharge my emotional batteries. When I know I am discharging too quickly, I take time out to recharge. I try to start my day with a full charge, often walking the dogs at "zero dark thirty," in the early AM. Much of the reason for this attention to particular coping mechanisms and stress reducers is that I often work in an extraverted world. I speak publicly, I preach, I teach. I am in meetings, on boards, and in committees. For an introvert, I do a lot of extraverted things. That does not make me any less an introvert. I would rather curl up with a good book or movie than go to a party. I know my personality, so I know my emotional strengths and limitations, and how to respond to situations that arise. I have friends that support and nurture me while holding me accountable. I have found healthy practices that I can do to alleviate stress, to cope. Even my faith has both private and public facets to it. I pray. I let myself be prayed over. I find refuge in my faith. I can tailor my activities, and therefore my response, to the stressful situation arising. And that means I do not live under stress.

Take Aways

It helps to know oneself. To know one's personality type can affect recovery. It does directly affect which types of stress reducers we choose, the mechanisms for how we cope with, and the methods of how we recharge our emotional and physical batteries. If we work with Veterans, it is good to get to know them to see what works with their personality.

Chapter 14

THEOLOGY

Theology

While AA is now secular, the founders freely spoke about their own spiritual experiences and their faith in God. The "Big Book" from Alcoholics Anonymous discusses faith and submission or surrender in a Higher Power, and names it, by stating, "… we had to fearlessly face the proposition that either God is everything or else He is nothing. God either is, or He isn't. What was our choice to be?"[132] This states that God is the Higher Power. John Baker echoes this when he says, "You will never know that God is all you need until God is all you get."[133]

Jürgen Moltmann speaks of being transformed into the *Imago Dei*, the image of God, "When the crucified Jesus is called the 'image of the invisible God,' the meaning is that

---

[132] Alcoholics Anonymous , 53.

[133] John Baker, *Your First Step to Celebrate Victory: How God Can Heal Your Life*. (Grand Rapids, MI: Zondervan, 2012), 244.

this is God, and God is like us."[134] This concept of God the Son suffering is further clarified, "And therefore, the suffering of abandonment is overcome by the suffering of love, which is not afraid of what is sick and ugly, but accepts it and takes it to itself in order to heal it."[135] What attracts converts to Christ is this theology of suffering, "To the extent that men in misery feel his solidarity with them, their solidarity with his suffering brings them out of their situation."[136] Even God suffers, "It is the unconditional and therefore boundless love which proceeds from the grief of the Father and the dying of the Son and reaches forsaken men in order to create in them the possibility and the force of new life."[137] Suffering, then, can not only be used for good, but can be necessary for true unconditional, or *agape,* love to come forth,

> He suffers because he lives, and he is alive because he loves. The person who can no longer love, even himself, no longer suffers, for he is without grief, without feeling and indifferent. Therefore the one who loves becomes vulnerable, can be hurt and disappointed. Where we suffer because we love, God suffers in us."[138]

---

[134] Jürgen Moltmann, *The Crucified God: the Cross of Christ As the Foundation and Criticism of Christian Theology.* (Minneapolis, MN: Augsburg Fortress Publishers, 1983), 205.

[135] Ibid., 46.

[136]Ibid., 51.

[137] Ibid., 245.

[138] Ibid., 253.

Dietrich Bonhoeffer speaks similarly of being conformed to Christ, "and thus to be everything that God created him to be."[139] This means that we must be willing to suffer, "... he must drink of the earthly cup to the dregs, and only in his doing so is the crucified and risen Lord with him, and he crucified and risen with Christ."[140] It is the Resurrection that makes the suffering worthwhile.

This echoes Schillebeeckx's theology of suffering, for a cause, for others. There is strength in tying our suffering to that of Christ on the cross, and to that of God suffering watching him die. Ken Williams notes that a purpose of suffering is, "To share in Christ's sufferings, becoming like Him in His death."[141] This echoes Moltmann's thought of being transformed into the *Imago Dei*.

Frankl saw a meaning, even a beauty in suffering, but more for what could be learned rather than for being transformed to the *Imago Dei*. While not a theologian but rather a psychiatrist asking existential questions, he still gets to the root of the problem, as noted earlier, "If there is meaning in life at all, then

---

[139] Michael Van Dyke, *Radical Integrity: The Story of Dietrich Bonhoeffer*. (Uhrichsville, OH: Barbour Publishing, 2001), 178.

[140] Dietrich Bonhoeffer, *Letters and Papers from Prison*. Enlarged ed. (NY: SCM Press, 1971), 337.

[141] Ken Williams, "Toward a Biblical Theology of Suffering," http://www.google.com/search/q=theology+of+suffering&hl=en&safe=active&gbv=2&gs-l=serp.1.0.0j0i303l3j0i22l2.10110.10110.0.13922.1.1.0.0.0.219.219.2-0.0.1.0.0FeVvKueK4VM&oq=theology=of+suffering, 4, (Accessed July 10, 2012.)

there must be meaning in suffering."[142] He might have agreed with Schillebeeckx in suffering for a cause.

Community

Brueggemann speaks of prophets that remind the community both of their shared history and of their future together, all in and through God. He tells us, in his preface to *Prophetic Imagination,* what the community needs to "raise up prophets." These are as follows: a long and available memory, an expressed sense of pain, an active practice of hope, and an effective mode of discourse.[143] Brueggemann has expressed these themes before in other works, especially the idea of a communal cry of pain that serves as both an accepted release and lessening from pain and a foundation from which hope arises.[144]

This communal cry of pain helps to frame the individual suffering. Brueggemann uses the Exodus from Egypt as a backdrop to subsuming the individual in and to the society. He says, "Israel's self-identity is from the outset a public one. From the beginning, personal life is experienced as participation in and appropriation of the public realities of oppression and pain."[145] The result? Brueggemann explains, "As Israel tells its faith-forming narrative, the pain is received, resolved, and honored

---

[142] Victor E. Frankl, 67.

[143] Walter Brueggemann, *The Prophetic Imagination.* 2nd ed. (Minneapolis: Fortress Press, 2001), xvi.

[144] Walter Brueggemann, *Hope Within History,* 24.

[145] Ibid., 11.

by Yahweh, the Lord of the Exodus...."[146] Because we can see the pain of the individual and the community's response as a community, we can extrapolate to the current: what is our society's collective response to the individual sufferer of PTSD? For it is the individual who suffers individually, as part of the community, and, more importantly, on behalf of the community. Therefore, there needs to be a communal response, a veritable communal cry of pain. The prophetic voice that arises from these conditions has as its purpose "to nurture, nourish, and evoke a consciousness and perception alternative"[147] to the current dominant consciousness of the culture.

On a societal or cultural level, Tick argues that we have a quasi-warrior society. The entry point into this culture is Boot Camp. The reminders of the former life are taken away (hair, clothes, jewelry, and control over waking, bathing, dressing, and sleeping) and are being overwritten with the attributes of a new culture (uniformity, shared experience, devotion to duty, and obedience). Of this enculturation, Tick adds, "The second essential component for making wars is constructed around one very simple rule: kill the other before he kills you."[148] Herein is where we as a society fail the individual. Where other warrior societies, such as the Samurai of Japan or the Native Americans of the Western Plains of the U.S., had mechanisms to deal with all aspects of life, Boot Camp may be the initiatory and only such experience of the modern U.S. warrior. Upon returning from deployment to a war zone, there may not be much societal

---

[146] Ibid., 18.

[147] Walter Brueggemann, *The Prophetic Imagination*, 3.

[148] Tick, 87.

input, other than perhaps a parade and "Welcome Home" events. Tick emphasizes, "If and when soldiers do return after perhaps some initial fanfare they are expected to reintegrate into mainstream consumer culture with little or no help."[149]

Thus arises the solitary Veteran, a warrior who isolates and insulates. *Isolation* is when an individual prefers their own company to others'. There are isolated communities in Texas 300 miles from the nearest VA. In these windswept arid locales, people go there to hide themselves from Life. As a chaplain, I traveled there to find these Veterans and to bring together local, state, federal, and non-governmental organizations and agencies to share our resources to help these Veterans.

Not only do Veterans isolate, they also tend to insulate. *Insulation* is when people surround themselves with others just like themselves. While this can be peer-to-peer support, it can also devolve into an Us vs Them mentality, where even family can move from Us and become Them. In both these situations, Isolation and Insulation, there is no streaming of fresh thoughts, no fresh wind of different experiences, no voices but those similar to one's own, who often are also struggling to make sense of the circumstance and have no answer. It can be the blind leading the blind. It is often a stagnant sea, with no healthy outlet, and nothing fresh coming in. To heal, we need a fresh wind: new thoughts, new experiences, new friends, new purpose. To heal holistically, we need Faith, Family, and Friends, in Community. More on this in a Chapter 17.

There are Veteran organizations such as the American Legion (AL), Veterans of Foreign Wars (VFW), Purple Heart Society, and Disabled American Veterans (DAV), to name a few,

---

[149] Ibid., 65.

but they are voluntary independent organizations. Voluntary, not mandatory, so not a society-wide membership. Secular, not theological, so the Veteran may not get all the help he needs. Another issue may be that often the VFW Hall or AL Hall often serves alcohol. When a Veteran self-medicates through alcohol, PTSD may not be fully addressed, just medicated over. The result is that our Veterans have untreated PTSD, which Tick defines as "a constellation of fixated experience, delayed growth, devastated character, interrupted initiation, and unsupported recovery."[150] In order to help our Veterans, which is to help our society, could we model both our treatment of PTSD and of being a Veteran, to the concept of an integrated warrior society, by at the least, having culturally supported recovery programs? Currently, these support groups listed are voluntary, are groups rather than one-on-one (therefore for extraverts), and, for those groups within the Vet Center,[151] are prohibited from identifying its clientele, which can hurt or help the Veteran.

While some may argue that this is best done by government, there is a compelling argument, backed by some of the resources already mentioned, that says churches and other private sources are better suited to meeting the needs of a mobile society. The Church (all Christian churches) centers its role in Faith, becoming the new Family and new Friends to effect

---

[150] Ibid., 107.

[151] The Vet Center Program was established by Congress in 1979 out of the recognition that a significant number of Vietnam era Vets were still experiencing readjustment problems, and had fears of reporting those problems. It is now for all Veterans, and is confidential. Some services are also available to family members.

healing. The Church is Community. And as has been discussed, there is healing in Community.

An example of this is found in Luke 10:30-37, in the passage commonly called the Good Samaritan. Jesus asks, "Who is your neighbor?" The characters are upright citizens; they are not the good neighbors. It is the outcast who is a good neighbor by tending the hurt and wounded. There is one other character: the innkeeper who welcomes those hurt and wounded. This is hospitality; this is Community.

Take Aways

We tend to Isolate, separate ourselves from others. We also tend to Insulate by grouping with others with similar experiences to ourselves. This often means an Us vs Them mentality, where even family becomes Them. The answer lies in Community, which is one reason the Church exists. Community is where faith, family, and friends intersect.

Chapter 15

TREATMENT MODALITIES

Treatment Modalities

There are three types of treatment modalities we will look at: those based on biology, those that are based in psychology, and those that are spiritually-based.

Biology

Generally, there are three biological models that help explain PTSD–SUD co-morbidity. Bryce Hruska and Douglas Delahanty list them, "… the self-medication hypothesis, the substance-induced anxiety enhancement hypothesis, and the shared vulnerability hypothesis."[152] The first model focuses on PTSD leading to SUD; the second model inverts that; the third model suggests that they both occur about the same

---

[152] Bryce Hruska and Douglas Delahanty, "PTSD-SUD Biological Mechanisms: Self-Medication and Beyond," ed. Paige Ouimette and Pamela P. Read. *Trauma and Substance Abuse: Causes, Consequences, and Treatment of Comorbid Disorders.* 2nd ed. (Washington, D.C.: American Psychological Association, 2014), 36.

time. D. Scott McLeod, in looking at male-male twin pairs in which both members served in the military, seems to dismiss the first two models, "Taken together, these findings suggest that the self-medication hypothesis does not explain either the association between PTSD symptoms and alcohol use or between combat and alcohol use."[153] This goes against what Wasdin experienced, as quoted earlier, "When you hurt on so many levels, alcohol-induced numbness becomes addictive." It also goes against many of my own experiences working with Veterans, many of whom drank so they could quiet their minds enough to sleep. To quote again the unnamed Veteran from page 2, "I have nightmares. I drink so I can sleep." They drank to either not remember or to forget, at least temporarily.

Initially McLeod seems to favor the third model, while dismissing genetic factors,

> These findings are most consistent with the shared vulnerability hypothesis in that combat exposure, PTSD symptoms, and alcohol use are associated because some portion of the genes that influence vulnerability to combat also influence vulnerability to alcohol consumption and to PTSD symptoms. Specific unique environmental factors were, however, more important than genetic factors for PTSD symptoms and for current alcohol use.[154]

---

[153] D. Scott McLeod, 272.

[154] Ibid., 270.

My experience, both before and after my research, suggests that there is a limited form of the self-medication hypothesis: some Veterans with intrusive PTSD memories may find their PTSD to be a cause of some SUD, which is then used as a coping mechanism by helping them either to forget or to not remember. Eventually the coping mechanism becomes another problem, which masks the original problem.

Psychology

Current psychological models for treatment revolve around empirically-based treatments. While each of these modalities require expertise, there is a discussion, especially around concurrent treatment, of using a care-team model, which "… does not require the individual practitioner to develop the type of expertise in multiple domains that may be difficult given finite resources for training and education available in some areas."[155]

Barbara Rothbaum, et al, reports,

> Cognitive-behavior therapy (CBT), a set of techniques that are directive, problem-focused, and delivered short term, is the psychotherapy approach with the most empirical support for its effectiveness. All the treatment

---

[155] Jay A. Morrison, Erin C. Berenz, and Scott E. Coffey, "Exposure-Based, Trauma-Focused Treatment for Comorbid PTSD-SUD," In *Trauma and Substance Abuse: Causes, Consequences, and Treatment of Comorbid Disorders*, ed. Paige Ouimette and Pamela P. Read. 2nd ed. (Washington, D.C.: American Psychological Association, 2014), 272.

guidelines for PTSD recommend CBT for
PTSD. The CBT technique with the most evidence for its efficacy ... is exposure therapy,
in which patients are aided in confronting the
trauma-related memories and cues in a therapeutic manner.[156]

CBT can be used as a stand-alone model. Chaplains are
not included in the delivery of the therapy, although they may
be consulted as needed external to the therapy.

A variation of CBT is Integrated Cognitive Behavioral
Therapy, or ICBT. Barbara Hermann, et al, explains,
"Treatment consists of psychoeducation linking PTSD and
SUD, breathing retraining, and cognitive restructuring."[157]
She concludes with, "... ICBT may be best suited for patients
with more severe PTSD and non-alcohol SUD; however, a
larger trial is needed."[158]

While CBT is the therapy with the most evidence, it is not
the only one. It focuses on treatment after the event. Some
focus on early intervention. Joseph Ruzek explains, "Early

---

[156] Barbara O. Rothbaum, Maryrose Gerardi, Bekh Bradley, and Matthew
J. Friedman , "Evidence-Based Treatments for Posttraumatic Stress
Disorder in Operation Enduring Freedom and Operation Iraqi Freedom
Military Personnel," In *Caring for Veterans with Deployment-Related
Stress Disorders: Iraq, Afghanistan, and Beyond*, ed. Josef I. Ruzek, Paula
P. Schnurr, Jennifer J. Vasterling, and Matthew J. Friedman. (Washington,
D.C.: American Psychological Association, 2011), 219.

[157] Barbara A. Hermann, Jessica L. Hamblen, Nancy C. Bernady, and Paula
P. Schnurr, "Evaluating the Evidence for PTSD-SUD Treatment," In
*Trauma and Substance Abuse: Causes, Consequences, and Treatment of
Comorbid Disorders*, 239.

[158] Ibid., 239.

intervention routinely includes the encouragement of basic care components such as rest, recreation, return to normal routines and roles, mutual social support, and education of survivors and families."[159]

Other programs deal with prevention intervention. One such model is in use by the military, the Stress Continuum Model. William Nash explains,

> The stress continuum model is a heuristic tool developed in the Marine Corps to provide a framework for prevention intervention across their spectrum. It categorizes all possible stress states into one of four color-coded stress zones.

> The two ends of the stress continuum are easily defined and well known. The Green 'Ready' Zone, to the left end of the continuum, is the zone of low or absent distress or dysfunction due to stress; it is the zone of wellness and resistance to current stress load. The Red 'Ill' Zone, to the far right of the continuum, is the zone of diagnosable stress-related mental disorders such as PTSD, depression, and substance abuse.

> The Yellow 'Reacting' Zone is defined as the stress zone of normal, common, and transient states of distress or changes in functioning.

---

[159] Joseph I. Ruzek, and Patricia Watson, "Early Intervention to Prevent PTSD and Other Trauma-Related Problems," *NC-PTSD Quarterly*, 4, Vol 12, (Fall 2001): 3.

Yellow Zone stress reactions, by definition, always disappear as soon as the stress is removed.

Yellow Zone stress reactions are not only normal but necessary, because such states of strain are essential to the development of greater capacity and competence, whether physical, mental, social, or spiritual.

In contrast, the Orange 'Injured' Zone is the zone of more severe and persistent states of distress or alterations in functioning, conceived to be caused by one of four stressor types: (a) life threat, (b) loss, (c) moral injury, or (d) cumulative wear-and-tear from many stressors over a prolonged period of time. [160]

One interesting thing about this model is that chaplains are included at every level of this treatment, often as part of a multidisciplinary team approach. This affords an opportunity to have an integrated approach, early on in the treatment, focused on the individual.

---

[160] William P. Nash, Lillian Krantz, Nathan Stein, Richard J. Westphal, and Bret Litz, "Comprehensive Soldier Fitness, Battlemind, and the Stress Continuum Model: Military Organizational Approaches to Prevention," In *Caring for Veterans with Deployment-Related Stress Disorders: Iraq, Afghanistan, and Beyond,* 205.

A different set of models receiving recognition use a stage–based framework. These use Judith Herman's model[161]: Stage 1: Safety; Stage 2: Mourning and Remembrance; Stage 3: Reconnection. One such model is Seeking Safety (SS), developed by Lisa M. Najavits. It "prioritizes stabilizing the patient, teaching coping skills, and reducing the most destructive symptoms."[162]

While Seeking Safety is a Stage 1 model focusing on the present, Creating Change (CC), is a Stage 2 model, focusing on the past, also developed by Najavits. This model is a therapy that can be used for both PTSD and SUD. There are several topics in each therapy. One of the differences between SS and CC is that, "… in SS each topic represents a safe coping skill; in CC, each topic represents a processing theme."[163] CC is the next step after SS, and the two models can be used separately or combined (sequentially, concurrently, or alternating).[164]

Another model is Acceptance and Commitment Therapy (ACT). Russ Harris informs us, "ACT gets its name from one of its core messages: accept what is out of your personal

---

[161] Judith Herman, *Trauma and Recovery*, (NY: Basic Books, 1997), 156.

[162] Barbara Hermann, Jessica L. Hamblen, Nancy C. Bernady, and Paula P. Schnurr, "Evaluating the Evidence for PTSD-SUD Treatment," In *Trauma and Substance Abuse: Causes, Consequences, and Treatment of Comorbid Disorders,* ed. Paige Ouimette and Pamela P. Read. 2nd ed. (Washington, D.C.: American Psychological Association, 2014), 240.

[163] Lisa M. Najavits, "Creating Change: A New Past-Focused Model for Trauma and Substance Abuse," In *Trauma and Substance Abuse: Causes, Consequences, and Treatment of Comorbid Disorders,* 296.

[164] Lisa M. Najavits and Kay M. Johnson, "Pilot Study of Creating Change, a New Past Focused Model for PTSD and Substance Abuse," *The American Journal on Addictions,* XX, (2014): 2.

control, and commit to taking action that enriches your life. The aim of ACT is to help us create a rich, full, and meaningful life, while accepting the pain that life inevitably brings."[165] To help accomplish this, Harris teaches, "The six core therapeutic processes in ACT are contacting the present moment, defusion, acceptance, self-as- context, values, and committed action."[166] Harris explains acceptance versus control, "ACT advocates acceptance under two circumstances:

1. When control of thoughts and feelings is limited or impossible.

2. When control of thoughts and feelings is possible, but the methods used reduce quality of life."[167]

This is precisely why ACT may be a therapy for addictions, "Many addictions begin as an attempt to avoid or get rid of unwanted thoughts or feelings...."[168] This may also work with PTSD, since many dealing with enormous trauma are persons seeking to forget.

---

[165] Russ Harris, *ACT Made Simple: An Easy-to-Read Primer on Acceptance and Commitment Therapy*, (Oakland, CA: New Harbinger Publications, 2009), 2.

[166] Ibid., 9.

[167] Ibid., 26.

[168] Ibid., 24.

Spirituality

The VA has postulated spiritual strategies for the recovery of PTSD sufferers. A VA pamphlet[169] instructs us,

Spirituality may improve post-trauma outcomes through:

1. reduction of behavioral risks through healthy religious lifestyles (e.g. less drinking or smoking),

2. expanded social support through involvement in spiritual communities,

3. enhancement of coping skills and helpful ways of understanding trauma that result in meaning-making, and

4. physiological mechanisms such as activation of the 'relaxation response' through prayer or meditation. Feelings of isolation, loneliness, and depression related to grief and loss may be lessened by the social support of a spiritual community.

A traumatic event or events are also called signal events or sentinel events. These may acquire a different meaning over time. An example is the 23rd Psalm, where the line, "Yea, though I walk through the valley of the shadow of death, I shall fear no evil," may mean something different at different ages, based on one's experiences. Yet, the experience at 10 may still

---

[169] "Spirituality and Trauma: Professionals Working Together," 2.

be valid at the age of 20, 30, 40.… The difference is in the layers added to the meaning, to one's interpretation of the event that add or color meaning.

Sometimes this perspective allows for a fresh insight. Perhaps the sentinel event that caused the PTSD has led to spiritual growth through the contemplation of the event. That it may lead to spiritual growth involves many factors. Contemplation has to be based on how we relate to each other and recharge, as an introvert or extravert.

One theological approach to what Allen Clark calls Combat Faith Ministry in *Wounded Soldier, Healing Warrior,* is his Battle Plan for Victory, which is outlined over several pages.[170] It is an outline and excellent resource for what churches can do not just for hurting Veterans, but also for hurting individuals.

Another resource is *The Combat Trauma Healing Manual,* geared for the individual sufferer, leading the person through a mnemonic on studying the Bible, to putting on spiritual Kevlar, looking at the schemes of Satan, and finally to wearing a new identity—one in Christ. Chris Adsit tells us, "One very effective way to release the unprocessed emotions of the past, heal traumatic memories, and counteract some of the physiological consequences of your trauma, is to experience a more powerful episode.…"[171] An experience with Christ leads to, "… images, senses, feelings, actions, and meanings of the past

---

[170] Allen B. Clark, *Wounded Soldier, Healing Warrior,* (St Paul, MN: Zenith Press, 2007), 303-311.

[171] Chris Adsit, *The Combat Trauma Healing Manual: Christ-Centered Solutions for Combat Trauma.* (Newport News, VA: Military Ministry Press, 2007), 29.

are confronted, re-experienced, processed, released, and over-powered by this new episode with Jesus."[172] This is reframing experiences, over- writing the experiences with new meanings, replacing the negative value with a positive value.

The "Big Book" from Alcoholics Anonymous tells of this overwriting as an "emotional rearrangement" due to spiritual experience, "Ideas, emotions, and attitudes which were once the guiding forces of these men are suddenly cast to one side, and a completely new set of conceptions and motives begin to dominate them."[173] This emotional rearrangement may also be called "finding the new normal." We are not what we once were, but we have a voice with God in who we are to become. To go further, we have a voice in the man and woman of God we are to become. This echoes II Corinthians 5:17, "Therefore if anyone is in Christ, he is a new creature; the old things passed away; behold, new things have come."

We try to find meaning, not just in our future, but in our past. And, God does not let our past go to waste. He has "plans for me," as found in Jeremiah 29:11, "For I know the plans that I have for you," declares the Lord, "plans for welfare and not for calamity to give you a future and a hope," include my past, my present, and my future. As Allen Clark puts it, "This time of personal trauma and turmoil in my life forced me to examine the truth about my real world of the present—my situation as

---

[172] Ibid., 29.

[173] Alcoholics Anonymous, 27.

it now existed." [174] His conclusion? He finds, "My self-image was based on my value in God's eyes…."[175]

By typing in the words "Christian recovery program," a quick Google search of the Internet yields 12,900,000 hits. Scanning the list reveals this to be grouped into either recovery programs or treatment centers. Within my local area, two Christian recovery programs are available: Celebrate Recovery and Reformer's Unanimous.

Celebrate Recovery is a recovery program "from any hurt, habit, or hang-up," as John Baker, the founder says. It modifies the Twelve Steps found in AA, each step surrounding one Scripture passage. There are also eight recovery principles taken from the Beatitudes found in Matthew 5: 3-10.[176] There is a mnemonic, RECOVERY, to help participants remember the principles.

Reformers Unanimous, found at reformersrecovery.com, uses ten recovery principles,[177] focusing on memorizing Scripture. To assist in this, there is a motivational award system that its founder, Steve Curington, says is "evidence of a program that believes in acknowledging accomplishment and rewarding participation." This is done at every gathering. The title of the program comes from Romans 12:1-2, and the participants earn and progress to titles such as Transformer, Conformer, and Reformer.

---

[174] Allen B. Clark, 175.

[175] Ibid., 255.

[176] John Baker, 29.

[177] Steve Curington, "The Ten Principles," 2013 Reformers Unanimous Christian Addiction Recovery Program, http://reformersrecovery.com/10principles, (Accessed June 20, 2014.)

There are other websites that afford pastor the assistance he/she may require to help the Veteran. One is the VA's website devoted to PTSD, the National Center for PTSD (NCPTSD): www.ptsd.va.gov, through their PTSD Consultation Program. This free service for all VA employees and providers who treat Veterans outside of VA is available to answer questions and provide consultation related to PTSD. Another website is the Department of Defense Center of Excellence (DCoE) for Psychological Health and Traumatic Brain Injury: http:// dcoe.mil, which has information webinars, and links to social media that caregivers and Veterans can access. The HealthCare Chaplaincy Network: www.healthcarechaplaincy.org/, has a program for assisting Veterans: http://www.chaplaincarefor-veterans.org/; either the Veteran or the caregiver can access the information. Deborah Grassman's website on soul injury is also invaluable: www.soulinjury.org.

What can pastors do? The main thing is to listen. Drescher says, "My approach to Veterans, in a non-threatening, non-confrontational way, is to invite them in. I walk them through their values, new meaning for living, and allowing them to reflect on their own historic faith perspective to move forward."[178] Storytelling is important both for the Veteran and for the community. Tick agrees, but adds that the reason is, "Veterans' stories need to be told in a way that transfers the moral weight of the event from the individual to the community."[179] A caveat: know that stories born in combat are often upsetting to hear, and may be hard to stomach, bringing up emotions we did not

---

[178] Kent Drescher, interview.

[179] Edward Tick, 223.

anticipate. When one listens, try to maintain a poker face. Any emotions crossing a listener's face may distract the speaker from sharing anything substantive. This may curtail healing.

If confession, both private and public, is necessary, then being a confessor or referring to a confessor is also necessary. Many churches have, or at least can use, a Service of Reconciliation. The preparation for this public ceremony can uncover depths of sin, as well as the process for alleviating that sin. Confession is a moving forward, accepting the past while embracing the future. Using Worthington's acrostic as a template for spiritual growth may be a vital link in moving forward.

When PTSD is not addressed, it will continue to fester. The DSM-5 states, "Symptom recurrence and intensification may occur in response to reminders of the original trauma, ongoing life stressors, or newly experienced traumatic events. For older individuals, declining health, worsening cognitive functioning and social isolation may exacerbate PTSD symptoms."[180]

PTSD has been with humanity, probably as long as there have been wars. Past societies dealt with the pain, often as community. The future of PTSD may lie, partially, in the past. We owe our Veterans, as a society, a future in which the past does not overwhelm. While there have been advances in our understanding of our bodies and minds, sometimes there has been an over-emphasis on the new and unproven over the tried and true. Sometimes progress involves regress. Sometimes progress means to use what we know works. This is a call to look at what works, whether old or new.

---

[180] American Psychiatric Association, *DSM-5*, 277.

In this next section, we will see how the past, for some, may cloud their view of the future, and yet, for others, becomes only one of many filters with which to see the future.

Take Aways

There is assistance for those wanting to help PTSD sufferers using a theological approach. There are workbooks like *The Combat Trauma Healing Manual* and *Wounded Soldier, Healing Warrior*. Several Christian recovery programs are available, depending on the locale. There are numerous websites that offer free information.

Chapter 16

CONTEMPLATION

Contemplation

In trying to make sense of the traumatic event or events resulting in PTSD, it may lead some to a greater faith and practice, and lead others to a loss of faith and practice. A strengthening of faith may protect the individual from the more deleterious effects of PTSD. Spiritual growth seems to be evidenced through the contemplation of the sentinel event or events. It is this contemplation, often over a period of years, that gives one's PTSD meaning. It is interesting to note that in trying to make sense of the trauma, some may strengthen their faith, often because of the trauma. For many Veterans, this contemplation led to a deeper level of faith, although not without some considerations.

Cognitive

One consideration deals both with the cognitive and with identity. The cognitive may be an altering of assumptions, of the world, of the concept of fairness, and of God. If assumptions about these spheres are shattered, so that what was normal is no longer, then there is a quest for the "new normal". The "Big Book" of Alcoholic Anonymous refers to this process as "emotional rearrangement" due to a spiritual experience, "Ideas, emotions, and attitudes which were once the guiding forces of the lives of these men are cast to one side, and a completely new set of conceptions and motives begin to dominate them."[181]

This shattering may affect faith and faith practice. Hagar ter Kuile says, "Therefore, a shattering of these assumptions can be expected to impact an individual's religiosity."[182]

I asked many combat Veterans this question, "How, if at all, did your faith practice change because of your combat experience?" The responses were illuminating. One Veteran, we will call him Veteran B, said, "I feel that God abandoned me." This is a pretty common response, sometimes barring an active faith, a regular church attendance, maybe even blaming God for everything bad in the world. Conversely, Veteran E said, "I felt protected by God." He stated further that he had to drive through a riot,

> Right after we drove through that riot, I felt I was protected by God. During the riot, though, it was scary, adrenaline-pumping. It was only 60 seconds but it felt like an eternity. One thing that reaffirmed the protection of God, our vehicle

---

[181] Alcoholics Anonymous, 27.

[182] Hagar ter Kuile, and Thomas Ehring, "Predictors of Changes in Religiosity After Trauma: Trauma
Religiosity, and Posttraumatic Stress Disorder," *Psychological Trauma: Theory, Research, Practice, and Policy*, 4, Vol 6, (2014): 354.

was the only one that didn't have shattered windows. The next day we felt as if we had run the world's most insane PT test.

Veteran F said, "My faith practice has increased since my initial combat experience."

He continues,

> I have been on ten deployments over eight years, 500 combat missions, 100-120 ground assault missions with Special Operations Forces. Once I left conventional units and went to Special Forces, experiences were more intense. Targets we went after were not low-priority, low-risk firefights, our risk of encountering resistance to our presence was greatly increased. My combat experiences changed in that I saw God allow things He didn't necessarily want. Probably sometimes I shouldn't have lived—but I did. A few feet, a few inches, could have changed everything. Only way to reconcile that is God had chosen me for something. No other explanation.

Another Veteran, Veteran I, starts off with a faith response, "I did not know of a time I did not believe in Christ." He then explains his faith,

> Immediately after (combat) I was confused about what I had learned in church and what I had done in combat. This didn't keep me from

> trying to live a Christian life. ... Because some
> of my men got killed, I had the mindset that
> what I believed about Jesus didn't work. I have
> since learned that I was asking too much of
> Jesus. I thought He should protect us more, but
> then I realized He did not have as much control
> because the enemy wasn't on the same page.
> That was my way of thinking.

This response shows that he was trying to reconcile previous training (church) to later training (combat) to find a synthesis of action; in essence, a systematic practical theology. This working out of one's faith in the foxhole of reality, this conversation between God and self, is theological reflection in action. This may occur at the moment of the event, but often later when all the experiences are synthesized so they can be reconciled. The question one may ask may be, "What does this mean?"

For some Veterans, the trauma event or events is what shatters the normal. For others, it is leaving the environment and the physical location where, as one Veteran put it, "I was in my element. I felt alive." For others, it is the combination of the traumatic event happening in the line of duty, often in combat, contrasted with the realization that this way of life is no more. In other words, what was normal in no longer; the search is on for the new normal. This may set some adrift, where they feel abandoned, and never feel they will be complete again. It may be a half-hearted search.

Often, someone who is devastated by PTSD lives in the past. The event or events may imprison them in that time. Often when someone says, "My past defines me," they mean, "My past confines me." Ironically, they hold the keys to their release. They become their own jailers.

A large part of recovery from PTSD is discovering a new normal. This may be a life review, what in AA is Step 4, previously cited, as "a fearless and searching moral inventory" of both the events and the person.

Take Aways

We tend to think about our past. But some people get stuck in the past. If my past defines me, my past confines me. We are more than the sum of our past, of our pain, of our trauma, even of our addictions. For others, reflecting on the past allows them to filter and bring forward the things that are needed, while relinquishing what is not needed for the future to the dust bin of experience.

Chapter 17

MISSIO DEI

Missio Dei

The *missio dei* is the mission of God. What is the mission of God in regard to Veterans? How are Veterans different than non-Veterans? At the root level, we, each of us, are simply people who are suffering. What is the mission of God to people who suffer? To help relieve their suffering by pointing them to the God who delivers.

Missionality

If churches and congregations are indeed missional, that is, carrying out the mission of God, then this framework of interweaving faith, family, and friends can prove a useful model for churches to play an important role in PTSD recovery. Churches can integrate the Veteran by going where they are and addressing their needs. Some Veterans and families may be lonely, in a new town without friends. Some may have children that would welcome inclusion. For the families of those deployed, they might appreciate some handyman or dependable go-to person. Older couples could also be surrogate grandparents. Since the military attracts young people, the conception of what is older may be relative and may simply mean someone older than the one or ones ministered to. In essence, missionality is remembering that the families left behind also serve on a front line, often without support. We can become that support. Here are some ideas what a church can do if they have Veterans or are near a military base:

1. Serve a meal for troops or Veterans on special occasions: Memorial Day, Flag Day, Independence Day, and Veterans Day.

2. Serve a meal on random days (do check with the military for a calendar of activities.)

3. Adopt a military family, especially if military member is on deployment—this works for Veterans, too.

4. Host a Veteran's Day breakfast/lunch, or a Men's or Women's Prayer Breakfast, or a family meal in conjunction with an outreach event. People come because they are invited.

5. Do service projects with and for Veterans.

6. Place military members and Veterans on church prayer lists and bulletins.

Mission

King David confesses his deed, acknowledges his guilt, and sees the events unfolding as his penance. Listen to David's pleading, at the beginning of Psalm 51,

> Be gracious to me, O God, according to Your lovingkindness; According to the greatness of Your compassion blot out my transgressions. [2] Wash me thoroughly from my iniquity And cleanse me from my sin. [3] For I know my transgressions, And my sin is ever before me,

Then he asks this in verse 10, "Create in me a clean heart, O God, And renew a steadfast spirit within me." This is a yearning from his heart, to not live his life ruled by the past. The prophet Isaiah, in Isaiah 1:16b-17, has the answer,

> Cease to do evil,
> Learn to do good;
> Seek justice,
> Reprove the ruthless,
> Defend the orphan,
> Plead for the widow.

Veterans often need a mission, something that gives their life meaning, a reason to wake up. This is often more than just working for a paycheck. It can be a cause, something greater than themselves, befitting a greater good. Or, it can be just a paycheck.

Veteran F speaks about finding God's will for his life, and how that brings peace,

> I work with Veterans and kids, working with trauma through horses. That's my quiet time. God has given me a gift to communicate with horses and with people and help people create trust with horses and help them draw parallels with that animal and their life. I believe that's what He has called me to do and that's what I work on.

He has found a mission, a life's work: building bridges of trust. He uses equine therapy for this because it speaks to him, in some way. Equine therapy, really any pet therapy, has a way of focusing outside of ourselves, outside of our problems, making us responsible for some other living thing dependent on us, loving us unconditionally. It is hard to be self-absorbed when there is a beating heart with needs in front of us.

When Veterans were in the military, they were a part of something larger. Many Veterans report on the camaraderie experienced. Sometimes it is the deep friendship forged in the furnace of combat. Sometimes these relationships are stronger than blood relationships. They understand the words that Jesus spoke, written in John 15:13, "Greater love has no one than this, that one lay down his life for his friends." These are words written on their hearts, experienced by only a few. This forges a bond, a new family, that Veterans miss and often want to recreate. Veterans often volunteer to again be part of something larger than themselves.

The list given before to do *for* Veterans, often means more *to* Veterans if done *by* Veterans.

Family and friends

Based on the research literature already presented and discussed, there seems to be three areas of resiliency: faith, family, and friends. These are areas that spiritual providers, be they chaplains, clergy, or pastors, can address. While we cannot change the past dynamics of a family, we can educate and provide new venues to create the family of choice. AA is all about providing a resource for alcoholics (NA for addicts). Is this not a new family? What is church but a relational enterprise to improve relations between individuals, between the individual and the group, and between sufferer and God? Do not people go to church for fellowship? Is not the entry point often because they are asked? The answer to the above questions is: yes! Church often takes the role of family, especially if the family of birth is toxic.

Let us also not forget that often the bonds formed in the military are centered in shared experiences. This camaraderie is even more evident when individuals share combat experiences. If the shared experiences are combat-related, then this seems to be more important than even unit-affiliation. It follows that once that connection is severed by leaving the combat area, leaving the unit, and/or leaving active duty, what will follow is a loss. Individuals need to acknowledge that loss in order to be able to grieve that loss. So, if churches can be both simply a safe place to share that loss, but even more importantly, if churches can assemble several who have known the close affiliations of being comrades-in-arms, then that same safe place can become a home, a family.

Some of the churches in this community have reached out to the suffering Veterans, providing them open arms, a ready ear, and a welcoming smile. Providing a safe place where a sufferer can be vulnerable may, and probably will, go a long way toward healing.

Faith

Faith is something that can be addressed if we are willing to reframe the theology, as discussed earlier. Discussions about this go to the heart of our soul, our moral or spiritual center, where the soul injury resides. While not everyone will agree on the approach or the terms, the need for discussion is there. I pray we can assist that discussion.

Combined with Isaiah 1:16b-17 listed previously, there is a passage in James 1:27 that speaks to faith, "Pure and undefiled religion in the sight of our God and Father is this: to visit orphans and widows in their distress, and to keep oneself unstained by the world." These are words of mission, grounded in faith.

Let us remember the term "soul injury" as defined by Deborah Grassman, "the un- mourned grief and unforgiven guilt that sometimes lingers in war's aftermath."[183] If combat PTSD involves a transgressive or causal element: **combat PTSD = soul injury + PTSD**, then the spiritual model must include a spiritual dimension, for which chaplains, ministers, and clergy are in a unique place to provide relief from this

[183] Deborah Grassman.

spiritual malady precisely because they are who they are, i.e., chaplains not psychologists, and because they are visible in the community. The result is that they may be approached before a mental health worker is approached, and often are.

A faith community has the unique place that models faith as necessary for holistic health, peace, and a joy-filled life. Chaplains, ministers, and clergy can point to the God-who–walks alongside, to the One who grieves with us, and to the One who delivers. We can also point to, and be in conversation with, the broader Christian Church, as the corporate body of faith in action, of Christ lived out every day. We represent Christ, and often we re-present Christ in a new way, through relationship.

Compassion

Earlier, we discussed Brueggemann's discovery of a communal cry of pain, communal practices, and a subsuming of the individual into the Community. In some ways, this is expressed hospitality. An example of this is found in Luke 10:30-37, commonly called the Good Samaritan. We have several characters: the victim, the religious, and the Samaritan. It is easy to see the religious as not loving due to not seeing the stranger as a brother or a neighbor. We know we do not want to be seen as them. We often credit the Samaritan as Jesus giving succor to the outcast, the vulnerable, the unprivileged. We want Jesus to treat us this way. We may see ourselves in the victim. But there is another character: the innkeeper. He is charged with taking care of him (the victim) until the Samaritan returns. The Church, as a loving Community of Faith, is the innkeeper. This is more than hospitality, this is our communal faith in action.

I want to present this model: **Community: Faith, Friends, Family**. All of these are found and expressed through a loving Church representing Community. These three, faith, family, and friends, are the heart of where we as a faith community can intercede. I am convinced that this is the answer to counter the twin problems of Isolation and Insulation. This is what Christians do: we live out our faith, in community, in brotherhood and sisterhood. We are not perfect; we are broken vessels in recovery. But because God has reached us in our pain, we can then reach out to others in their pain. We can do this with empathy, a connecting of one's pain to another's pain, which is not just sympathy. We do this with compassion, literally "with passion," sharing a burden. A burden shared is a burden lessened. This is often accomplished by prayer. Are we not called to bathe the process, as well as the individual sufferer, in prayer? An example may be a public invitation for the community to gather for prayer for Veterans, for this nation, and for the consequences of war. A corporate confession may begin here. I gave a prayer at a Memorial Day event, which happened to be the 50th anniversary of the Vietnam War. Among other statements, I apologized for my generation and society's treatment of returning Vietnam servicemen and women. Afterwards, many of the Vietnam Veterans told me that hearing that one statement meant more to them than all the other speeches combined. They remembered nothing else about what I had said, except that I had apologized, a corporate apology, which they accepted.

Take Aways

Veterans often need a mission, something that gives their life meaning. They often volunteer to again be part of something larger than themselves. Service *to* Veterans often means more *if* done *by* Veterans. Community models Faith, Family, and Friends.

Chapter 18

IMAGO DEI

Imago Dei

T he *Imago Dei* is the image of God. If we are made in the image of God, can we see the image of God in ourselves? I refer back to Chapter 7: Identity for this discussion. Can we see it in someone else? What does it take to see this? In my work with SUD Veterans, I have found that many people suffer from a negative self-image, reinforced by family and society. Once they are labeled by the court system, the police, the VA, or family, it is hard to break the label. The concern for churches is how we see the sufferer. Do we see the wounded warrior as a victim mourning the loss of identity and as a future disciple to be embraced? Perhaps this is also how we should see those who suffer from PTSD.

Confession

Both Edward Tick and Robert Certain discuss what we can do after the event. Earlier, I quoted Certain, "Parades and medals provide a secular answer; confession and absolution provide the religious answer."[184] To be able to share, to confess in order to receive absolution, requires trust. Trust only comes from relationship. We as Christians model and mirror the Presence of Christ. We represent Christ, but sometimes we also need to re-present Christ in a new way, through relationship. Are there places where churches can be to provide the compassion of Christ? Yes: wherever it is that Veterans gather. Better: open the doors of the church to have those opportunities inside, where the attendees can be showered with love!

The purpose of individual confession, as David Belgum told us earlier, is to restore the dignity of the individual and return him or her to community and to God. This desire for restoration can only come about because something is broken, and that something is often a negative view of self. Brokenness does not necessarily have to be sin. Rather, it can be a disruption of the familiar based on one or several sentinel events that may be or are life-changing.

The purpose of corporate confession, as Walter Brueggemann told us, is to embrace the pain so as to foster hope, which then rebuilds faith. Jonathan Shay reminds us that only when the community embraces the collective pain, can the individual step outside the pain to begin healing.

This is what Walter Brueggemann and Edward Tick were referring to, where the individual can rest in a supportive community, a community that collectively shares the burden of the individual. This allows them to find meaning within the suffering as Victor Frankl and Edward Schillebeeckx discussed. Is

---

[184] Robert Certain, 275.

this possible? We can know only if we try, first as a community of faith in just one community.

Corporate confession is one way to express the inexpressible and, often, indefinable need to release the pain. When a faith community confesses, it builds trust in the affected community. Corporate confession to wars, how Veterans were treated, and compassion to Veterans' issues, builds bridges of trust to Veterans so Veterans can then trust the faith community with their individualized pain.

Resurrection

Larry Graham reminds us of a theology of Christian resurrection, often amid unmentionable and indescribable trauma and death. This offers hope. It is in facing the devastation that has been evidenced, both the effects and the causes, that allows us to focus on the God-who-walks-alongside, the God of hope and healing. And we, as a Community of faith, point to One who walks-alongside as we also endeavor to do so.

Chapter 19

PAIN

Listening to Pain

T here is a prison ministry, Kairos, that goes into prisons to minister to the prisoners. And how do they minster to them? They are guided by the dictum, "Listen, Listen, Love, Love". It was amazing to me when I realized that many people have never been listened to, *really* listened to. And then to include love, an unconditional love, that many have never experienced. These two factors, unaddressed, keep people from finding hope, peace, forgiveness, belonging, true love, and a future. I do not think I overstate this.

Pain, unaddressed, will continue. Veteran B said, "Pain is inevitable; misery is optional." Faith is what can remove the pain from the memory. Often this is through forgiveness: of self, of others, and of God. Many of the stories I hear center on the subject of unforgiveness. We know that once we accept the grace of forgiveness for ourselves and extend it forward toward others, we are free from the guilt, sin, and stain of the event.

This happens at that moment of acceptance of God's grace. Yet, we also recognize that for some, there may be a focus on feeling or emotions; without which, there is doubt. For them, I say, "When we can remember the event without the pain, we have achieved forgiveness." Not only the definition but the expression lived out. This is what the faith community can express with conviction. Using Worthington's six steps previously listed in Chapter Two as a template for spiritual growth may be a vital link in moving forward.

To interview someone is to listen. Moschella reminds that this is a pastoral practice, "Listening can be a means of grace, as it brings forth stories through which people make sense of their lives and become aware of the larger reality."[185]

Be prepared to listen. Be prepared to hear pain. When spiritual injury is involved, there is soul pain. There may be a mixture of emotions that are turbulent, waiting to burst.

The stories told in the previous chapters evoke soul pain and speak to our hearts. Each Veteran, indeed every person, has a story to tell. There is a thought common to hospice care that a person will continue to tell a story until they know they are heard. With each re-telling, the pain loses its grip on the wounded soul. Sometimes our role may be only to listen, to listen with our being. While the telling of painful events is itself painful, this is a pain of transition to something beyond, from unsafe to safe. This pain of transition is necessary to move away from the pain of PTSD.

Prayer

None of this can go forward without bathing the process, the individuals, and the care- givers in prayer. We have already

---

[185] Mary Clark Moschella, *Ethnography as a Pastoral Practice: An Introduction*, (Cleveland, Pilgrim Press, 2008), 144.

discussed the purpose of prayer: to know the mind of Christ and the will of God; to align oneself with that will; and to change hearts and situations (often this means that the heart of the one who prays is changed). All of these are worthy goals. But is that all? Is there more? Remember what Phineas F. Bresee said, "The aim of the prayer meeting is to get heaven open and the glory down." This speaks to the power of prayer, but also the purpose of prayer.

Prayer, at the most basic, is simply a conversation with God. Conversation, not monologue. A monologue consists of me telling God what I want. A conversation entails both speaking and listening. This is where the *purpose* of prayer is revealed. When we pray to God, we align our wills, our minds, and our hearts with His. This means He lives in us. When this happens, then God can speak to us, and we will listen and obey. The more subsumed my will is in His, the more I can listen, without distraction, and obey.

We often pray when prayer is all we have. We come in apparent weakness, but leave filled with power. II Corinthians 12:9 says, "And He has said to me, 'My grace is sufficient for you, for power is perfected in weakness.' Most gladly, therefore, I will rather boast about my weaknesses, so that the power of Christ may dwell in me."

We have discussed the *power* of prayer in Chapter 11: Prayer and know that prayer can change both hearts and situations. I cited both James 5:16 and Exodus 32:14. The passage in James tells us to confess to, and pray for, one another. The passage in Exodus is about intercessory prayer.

What is the *practice* of prayer? When do we pray? When we get up in the morning? When we go to bed to sleep? Throughout the day? The answer is, "Yes!" The time is not legalistic. It is rather when one finds the time to read the Bible, speak from the heart, and listen the same way. I have found that if I schedule my time, I can get in the habit of praying. I get used to doing something by doing it. The more I practice it, the easier it becomes, and the better I become at it.

When we pray, we take the focus off ourselves and place it onto God.

Take Aways

Listen, Listen, Love, Love. Many people have never experienced, really experienced, these terms. People suffer in pain. Faith is what can remove the pain from the memory. When we can remember the event without the pain, we have achieved forgiveness. Listening is hard work. We need to bathe the process in prayer before we listen. Prayer can change the focus from us to others, from inward to outward.

Chapter 20

EMOTIONS AND ACTIONS

Normative Behavior

B efore we talk about the title of this chapter, Emotions and Actions, we need to discuss normative behavior. While all emotions are natural, it is the intensity and duration of them that can be problematic.

One way to look at normative behavior is to study the mores of a society to determine what are the morals, what are the customs, and what are manners that are desired. One problem: which society? A motorcycle gang is different from a study group at college. The reality is that we often function in different societies at one time.

Another issue is that societies change over time. Our own society is vastly different now than it was 1000 years ago, moving from an agrarian society and feudal overlords to a complex national-international business model. Comparing 100 years ago to now the difference is staggering. Many years ago, I interviewed a WWI Veteran. Here are some of the things he saw and went through: horses to automobiles, steam locomotives to diesel trains, early bi-planes to jets, silent movies to color talkies, hand-cranked telephones with operators to mobile devices. Social media? Who knew? Even if it was just 50 years ago, 30 years ago, even 10 years ago, society has changed to the point where many feel lost and confused.

Is there a standard? We can go back in time to what was accepted in society, and in fact, still is the standard for some societal functions: formal dinners. A popular newspaper article, "Miss Manners", would answer questions about, well, manners. Emily Post wrote a book called *Rules for Etiquette*. But if there is not a formal dinner at the White House in our future, what is our standard of normative behavior?

Social media has answers. The answers are often not what we need to hear or do. They seem to be the, "Here, hold my beer," variety, which does not lead to good results. ERs and jail cells prove this, as do the unwanted tattoos the next day. Even if given with passion or innocence, ignorance is not the best teacher. When we discussed the concept of Insulation, it was the idea of a body of water with no fresh water source, with no filters, no movement, only stagnation. Our minds are the same way. Behavior and action follow what we think.

Peer-to-peer listening can be therapeutic. There is usually a moderator who has "been there" and gone on past the pain. He has overcome ignorance and can guide the participants. Peer-to-peer without a moderator is often the blind leading the blind, which does not often turn out well.

There was a well-known example that happened in Africa at a wild game park. Older elephants were hunted for their tusks, leaving the younger elephants without older role models. As they grew up, they became delinquents, tearing up the environment, causing ruckus, living by their own rules. They were teenagers, elephant teenagers. What to do? After long thought, the game wardens brought in an older male elephant from another park. This big bull was physically imposing, with the younger elephants literally looking up to him. Immediately, the teenagers quieted down and stopped their ruckus. Now they had a guide to follow and model. If it works for elephants, then....

We don't have bull elephants to guide us. Is there another option? A better option? What does the Bible say about normative behavior? Normative behavior, or right behavior, is that which pleases God. Right behavior is righteous, or holy, behavior. This is not "holier than thou", but simply, we do what is right because it is right. How do we determine that? We have three sources:

1. Study the Word of God. It gives examples, both good and bad, to learn from. It seeps into our minds, then hearts, and becomes a living guide.

2. Pray to God. As discussed before, prayer is both listening and speaking. Sometimes we really need to listen.

3. Submit to God. We discussed this as well. We are not teenagers anymore. We live in adult society. We need to submit ourselves to a higher authority, The Higher Authority, God.

When we accept and do all these three, we make better decisions, and we feel better about ourselves.

A slightly different view is when trauma occurs. The words and advice that follow may be taken as exceptions to right behavior. To again quote Victor Frankl, "An abnormal reaction to an abnormal situation is normal behavior."[186] Sometimes we have to think and do outside the box of normal behavior. It may be, or seem to be, the right thing to do at the time. The operative phrase is "at the time" or "for a time or season". We know that time passes and seasons change. This is a thorny issue. My sergeant often advised me, "It is better to be judged by 12 than carried by 6." Words for a different world than I encounter now. These words and advice are for a different world that we encounter rarely, perhaps only in the past. When we leave that world, we leave what was "normal" for there, and leave it there. We leave that situation in the past and enter this world where we now "do" society with new normative behavior patterns. While that behavior and thought process was normal for that situation, when we leave that situation we leave that behavior and thought processes behind to embrace something normal for the situation that we are now in. This is hard to apply for many people, but in reality, we do it all the time. Our behavior at a professional sports team game may be different that our behavior in church, which is not a bad thing. We change our behavior, what is normal, to fit the situation.

Emotions

We all have emotions, and sometimes, oftentimes, those emotions lead us to actions. Let me say again that all emotions are normal and good. What can be bad, and lead to bad situations, is the duration and frequency of those emotions. Anger can be good and can lead to change. Living in perpetual anger is not healthy, for anybody. It often erupts, and like a volcano, doesn't care where it goes.

When listening to stories, be prepared to hear things one may not have ever heard or never imagined, especially things that may make one aghast, but we need to hear to understand so we will not demonize the speaker, who is often themself a victim of their circumstances.

One Veteran told me this, "I woke up with my hands around my wife's throat. I was scared and left her and the kids. I left because I loved them." This is not an uncommon story. Veteran S also told me this had happened to him with a couple of girlfriends. I share these stories not to titillate but to inform, and to wonder. Imagine a child experiencing this. And then experiencing his father leave them, leave him, without explanation. "Does he not love me?" A child may take this as rejection, growing up with resentment. Now imagine this same child finding out the reason: fear. Now the child has a new set of emotions tied to memories to unravel. PTSD has many ripples, leaves many scars, sometimes for a lifetime.

Veteran S later said this about himself, "I was so built up in pride and confidence, then was crushed by my feebleness. Having to identify and own my frailty after being so sure of my being 10ft tall and bulletproof." To think that one emotion caused this chain of events is startling and sad. Could he have gotten help? Could we have found out what caused the blackout causing the current event, as well as the fear afterward? Yes, but it does take a lot of work, a lot of soul-searching, a lot of digging up memories and talking about them until the pain is not overwhelming. Re-telling lessens the trauma.

While we all have emotions, out time in the military shows that one emotion is prized above all others: anger. Anger is useful in combat situations, focusing the mind on one subject and forming tactics to surmount that problem. But, again, we cannot sustain anger for an indefinite period of time. We cannot live in anger. It is not healthy. The emotion leads to action, and actions born of anger rarely have good results.

What is the answer? When we discussed personality in a previous chapter, we learned that according to Myers-Briggs, we lean to either an introverted or an extraverted nature. We learned that we naturally favor activities that cater to our nature. I related that I am an introvert. As an introvert, I find activities to destress, to decompress, and to relax that I can do alone. Some of these include the following: physical activity, reading, walking, going to the park, riding a bike, playing with the dogs, etc.

What else? When in the middle of a situation, I say a quick centering prayer, praying for peace, clarity of mind, and the right words to say and action to take. If I can recite Scripture as a prayer, all the better, e.g., "'I can do all things through Christ who strengthens me!' Philippians 4:13. Amen." I call these breath prayers, a prayer I can do in one breath.

If I can leave the situation, then a quick walk to clear the mind and emotions. While I am not recommending a smoking break, I want to break down what actually happens in these breaks. Since many buildings and some cities no longer permit smoking inside, then movement is required. First, one leaves the site, leaving the equipment and one's focus there, then moving to another site. If using an elevator or taking the stairs, it's a change of scenery, with maybe some activity. When one arrives at the destination, usually outside, there is new scenery plus smells, perhaps of flowers, a feeling of wind upon the skin, the sight of skies, clouds, and sun. Perhaps one chats with co-workers. Then one lights up, a very small part of this whole process. The majority of the time is spent doing other activities. This is transferrable. Call it a non-smoking break.

One major thing I do is prepare myself. I know my limits. If I am driving, and someone tailgates me, I have several options.

I can turn the windshield blue with choice words. I can retaliate. The news is full of these tragedies. Or I can bless. Blessing someone is calling forth what is hidden. We bless a politician with integrity. We know he has it in him, somewhere. We just want it to show. With a driver who is an EGR (Extra Grace Required), I bless them with peace, God's peace. But, and this is also important, I take my foot off the accelerator, put some distance between us, and move over into another lane. If the EGR driver is going to have a wreck, I do not want to be anywhere close. Blessing them allows me to breathe in Peace. In fact, I get a blessing too from blessing others. It is as though a small portion is returned to me. If the blessing is received, one less wreck, as well. This practice is called the "Art of Blessing".

Preparing myself also means having a support system. Whether it is an individual or a group, it helps to share successes as well as needs, praises as well as prayer needs, venting at a soundboard as well as needing advice. Admit it: we cannot do it alone well all the time. It is no sign of weakness to admit this fact of human nature.

I also have a support structure with my family. They also served on the front lines on the home front. We have been through good times and bad but have stuck together, getting stronger along the way. The reason for this unity is due to faith. We share a faith, tried by circumstance, strengthened by the same circumstance, and sown in love. I say this because this mindset is a process that takes time, time many do not have. If someone gets married, then a month or two later deploys, then time is a luxury they do not/did not have.

These last three are vital to continued recovery from trauma, from incidental instances of anger, or just as a general prophylactic against a bad day. These three: Family, Friends, and Faith, are found in families of blood or families of choice. Some have burned bridges with family. New bridges can be built with a family of choice. To find those new bridges, to form new family, to have new friends, to inculcate a faith, this is what I have found to be the sustainable antidote to trauma. Let me go further. Since I am a Christian chaplain, I use a Christian approach, steeped in Scripture. I realize there are other faith traditions, but I know what works for me and for those I counsel. God can heal. That is one of His names: Yahweh Rapha, The Lord God Who Heals.

Actions

If we will what we believe or perceive, then emotions begin in the mind, and the result of our emotions come out as actions. If those actions end up being commissions of sin, or even sinful omissions, then forgiveness is needed, as we discussed in Chapter 9: Forgiveness.

For all other actions, we need to consider our mindset. If we do not want resultant actions we later regret, we first need to adjust the way we think. We have a choice in what we do; we have a choice in what we think. What are you thinking of? If I fill my mind with dark images, then I may do dark things. Or it may be as simple as waking up deciding to have a good day. Self-fulfilling prophecy says we will have the day we envision. If I tell myself I will have a bad day, I probably will. I will find fault with others, question their motives, think the worst, maybe even get mad easily and vocally. If I tell myself I will have a good day, I probably will. I will look for the good in people, forgive easily, laugh more. I determine this when I wake up. When I roll over and see my wife, I can choose to love her, or

I can choose not to. Whatever I choose, I will do. If love is a choice of the will, then all other emotions and resulting actions are also. Control that mindset. That we can do.

The paragraphs listed above where we discussed Faith, Family, and Friends, works not just on emotions but also on actions. We can prevent bad actions by having an outlet ahead of time. Discussing how we see and react to stressors and getting feedback from trusted sources may affect how we engage the next stressor. Role models are also effective at any age. These are prophylactic measures that are encouraged and wholesome. Remember also that emotions precede actions.

Within this chapter, on the subchapter on Emotions, I referenced Veteran S. He had experienced something so traumatic, what he had seen and what he had done, that it infiltrated his dreams, so that his reality was altered. His sleep reality woke him up with this reality intruding itself on his wakeful reality. He woke up realizing he was choking his girlfriend. Unfortunately, it happened more than once. As he said, "It happened to two girlfriends." It was obviously something he could not control. He tried various measures, to no avail. It wasn't until he surrendered himself to Christ, found a church where he could be surrounded by a support group of caring, listening individuals, and come to trust God, that his faith in Christ healed him. He is now studying for the ministry. It has been a long road.

We had already discussed the effects of support of family and friends on past actions. The more the stories of our actions are talked about, the less the impact the past holds over our present and our future, and the more healing occurs. Taken together, then a support group of family and friends can influence actions past, present, and future.

Another thing that can influence actions is the paragraph above on blessings. Just as blessings can influence the actions of others, blessings can also influence our own actions. Listen to the words of Jabez found in I Chronicles 4:10,

Now Jabez called on the God of Israel, saying, "Oh that You would bless me indeed and enlarge my border, and that Your hand might be with me, and that You would keep *me* from harm that *it* may not pain me!" And God granted him what he requested.

This passage above is found in a listing of generations. Suddenly this passage pops up. When this happens, when a flow of information is interrupted, that means it is important. The way it ends, "And God granted him what he requested," is also important. I often quote from and modify this passage, "Lord bless me indeed, let Your hand be on me, and keep me from harm, either giving or receiving."

Take Aways

While all emotions are natural, it is the intensity and duration of them that can be problematic. Behavior and action follow what we think. Normative behavior, or right behavior, is that which pleases God. We leave certain situations in the past to enter this world where we now "do" society with new normative behavior patterns. While that behavior and thought process was normal for that situation, when we leave that situation we leave that behavior and thought processes behind to embrace something normal for the situation that we are now in. Practice the "Art of Blessing", including blessing yourself.

Chapter 21

SPIRITUAL RECOVERY PROGRAMS

Safe places

Sufferers need to meet in safe places. This is another area where churches and ministries can help in recovery is providing sanctuaries, or safe places. Carrie Doehring says, "Recovery involves first creating safety and trust...."[186] It is in these safe harbors that rituals may be of use. Tick states, "Warriors need elaborate rituals cleansing them of pain and stain."[187] He then outlines "four essential steps: purification and cleansing; story-telling; restitution in the family and the nation; and initiation as a warrior."[188] Of the first step, he advocates a Native American sweat lodge for some. But he warns, "These are best done by ritual in the context of a supportive community."[189]

---

[186] Carrie Doehring, *Internal Desecration: Traumatization and Representations of God.* (Lanham, MD: University Press of America, 1991), 137.

[187] Edward Tick, 102

[188] Ibid., 189.

[189] Ibid., 211.

To move from the unsafe to the safe involves transition. I John 2:8 discusses transition points, "… the darkness is passing away and the true Light is already shining." The church can recognize that transition points between expected reality and actual reality are traumatic. Yet, this pain of transition is necessary to move away from the pain of PTSD. Change is often dangerous simply because it involves a change from the familiar.

There is ministry in the liminal space between safe and unsafe. This is a transition point, crucial in reaching the Veteran, and crucial for the Veteran.

Churches can host AA/NA meetings. Churches can also get involved in spiritual recovery programs, such as Celebrate Recovery and Reformer's Unanimous, to either complement or replace existing AA programs. Interestingly, the approaches used by these programs can be applied equally to PTSD and SUD. Celebrate Recovery goes further, and says that we each have hurts, hang-ups, and habits that we need God to deal with. These recovery programs provide a theological underpinning to recovery.

Because of the sheer number of Veterans diagnosed with PTSD who are not being reached through the available channels, the VA has begun building bridges between mental health and chaplaincy. This is something that churches could do in, and for, the community. Churches can collaborate with the various mental health services that are available to reach and help the Veteran who suffers by offering programs, by listing their affiliation with various agencies, and by having trained people on staff to listen and refer. This also means building these bridges long before a crisis happens.

Sponsors

Veterans in recovery tell me they need sponsors. Sponsors are safe places, in the form of people, to whom the darkest recesses of one's heart can be opened and shared. Many Veterans beginning recovery face the same issues: denial, anger, cognitive dissonance, broken relationships, loss of hope, mistrust, financial issues, legal issues, and residence issues (homelessness). When a Veteran loses trust in humanity, mere words will not restore the trust. A sponsor is someone who can be trusted, who can build or rebuild trust, who can be called on at any time of the night. Is this not a definition of discipleship, of Christianity in action, of being Christ to someone?

Toolbox

PTSD has been around since the first conflict. I find it interesting, even freeing, that the modern problem of PTSD has an answer in the history of God's chosen people. Walter Brueggemann points to the Exodus, when the whole nation was at war, with every family sending forth a warrior. The families received the warrior back, either living or dead. But the way they dealt with the trauma, the grief, and the loss is what is radical: Community. It is radical because we do not do it. They had a community of faith where everyone felt a sense of belonging. This is the answer! We can be Community! What we have forgotten, we can remember. What we can remember, we can implement. What we can implement, can change society for the better.

Everett Worthington's six steps for moral repair through self-forgiveness, Allen Clark's Battle Plan for Victory, and

Chris Adsit's *The Combat Trauma Healing Manual: Christ-Centered Solutions for Combat Trauma,* all discussed previously, are tools that any follower of Christ interested in working with Veterans with combat PTSD should have in their toolbox.

I include these websites that I use and that can afford the pastor the assistance he/she may require to help the Veteran: Deborah Grassman's website on soul injury: www.soulinjury.org. (I have been in her workshops, purchased her books, and can recommend them.); the National Center for PTSD (NC-PTSD) website: www.ptsd.va.gov; the Department of Defense Center of Excellence (DCoE) for Psychological Health and Traumatic Brain Injury website: http://dcoe.mil; and the HealthCare Chaplaincy Network's Chaplain Care for Veterans website: http://www.chaplaincareforveterans.org/.

Take Aways

Many Veterans beginning recovery face the same issues: denial, anger, cognitive dissonance, broken relationships, loss of hope, mistrust, financial issues, legal issues, and residence issues (homelessness). The modern problem of PTSD has an answer in the history of God's chosen people. What we have forgotten, we can remember. What we can remember, we can implement. What we can implement, can change society for the better.

Chapter 22

WHAT'S NEXT

A braham Lincoln gave his Second Inaugural Address, on March 4, 1865, just 41 days before his assassination. Toward the end of his speech, he spoke these words, "...Let us strive on to finish the work we are in to bind up the nation's wounds, to care for him who shall have borne the battle and for his widow and his orphan...."[190] Since the reader is here because they want to be part of the process of healing, I want to modify those words I opened this book with by replacing "I" with "We": "We mourn for those that did not come home, celebrate with those that did, and minister to those who left something 'over there'. That which is left behind can be physical, relational, emotional, and/or spiritual." In accordance with Lincoln's words and my thoughts, I would look to the future, and how we are to respond to those who hurt.

---

[190] Abraham Lincoln, Lincoln's Second Inaugural Address, March 4, 1865, https://www.nps.gov/linc/learn/historyculture/lincoln-second-inaugural.htm Accessed September 9, 2022.

Future Research

Additional research needs to be conducted on a larger scale, with both sexes, on those with co-morbid diagnoses of SUD and PTSD. Local pastors, ministers, chaplains, and clergy are on the front line, but they are not alone. Local pastors, minsters, and those who work with Veterans can find and use the resources outlined in the various chapters in this book. I summarized the salient points of the research paper that was fundamental to this book and presented a webinar to the National VA Chaplains in April 2015, so that they would feel empowered to contact the local pastor and share resources.

It seems that it may be neither combat duration nor frequency, but rather combat experience and intensity, that may be the greater factors in whether faith and faith practice are impacted either negatively or positively.

There is a new scale, the Killing Combat Scale from the National Center for PTSD (NCPTSD). I have not used this scale, so I cannot attest to its effectiveness. But I have used both the Burns PTSD scale and the PCL-5 instruments and would like to see a large-scale research project using these instruments. The scale of my research was small, and yet, this small sample showed that recovery from PTSD without a faith component may not lead to a complete recovery. When a spiritual injury is present, recovery without a faith component may not even be possible. My experience with SUD Veterans suggests that while the AA program can be navigated without a spiritual component, relapse will usually occur. However, when a strong theological component is part of the treatment for SUD, then the healing of spiritual injury becomes much more likely. Since many of my patients that had SUD also had PTSD, I also expect similar results on spiritual injury healing when a strong theological component is present.

While working in a Level II Trauma Center's Emergency Room (ER) and Intensive Care Unit (ICU), followed by stints in Palliative and Hospice care, adding in a heartfelt tour and experience in a Neonatal Intensive Care Unit (NICU), as well as working with women in Abortion Recovery, I tried this theological approach. I found that what works with combat Veterans with PTSD also works with all, or most all, PTSD patients. And this brings to mind a whole bunch of questions, as well as possibilities, and perhaps, a whole new endeavor for me.

Why does a theological approach work with all, or most all, PTSD sufferers? Pain is universal. Pain speaks to pain. Therefore, one's experience with pain may connect with another's pain. The pain, traumatic event, or experience does not have to be exactly similar. If I can reach inside of me and experience my own pain, and in so doing connect with someone else's pain, then I have connected and ministered to someone suffering. There are undifferentiated approaches as well as differentiated approaches, based on the type of trauma. While there is a call for specialized approaches to the type of pain, general approaches seem to do well. While all trauma is different, there are also similarities, and theological, holistic therapies speak to those similarities of pain. Why? The answer is simply that God is the Great Healer of all pain.

Let me go further. PTSD is a wounding of the Spirit, both the Holy Spirit and the spirit of the individual. The overall Greek term for this is *Pneumatrauma,* the wounding of the Spirit. The field is called *Pneumatraumatology*, the study of the wounding of the Spirit. While this book focuses on combat trauma, i.e., trauma sustained while in combat, the truth is that what works for combat trauma works with trauma across the board. So, as you read this, apply the concepts to other types of trauma: rape, abortion, muggings, carjackings, car wrecks, acts of terrorism, etc. The issues Veterans face in overcoming the trauma of PTSD are often the same issues people face when overcoming other trauma, simply because we are human. Therefore, there is a commonality of reactions, feelings, thoughts, and behavior.

Take Aways

PTSD is a wounding of the Spirit, both the Holy Spirit and the spirit of the individual. I term this *pneumatrauma.* It seems that it may be neither combat duration nor frequency, but rather combat experience and intensity, that may be the greater factors in whether faith and faith practice are impacted either negatively or positively. While all trauma is different, there are also similarities, and theological, holistic therapies speak to those similarities of pain. Why? The answer is simply that God is the Great Healer of all pain. The truth is that what works for combat trauma works with trauma across the board. The issues Veterans face in overcoming the trauma of PTSD are often the same issues people face when overcoming other trauma, simply because we are human. Therefore, there is a commonality of reactions, feelings, thoughts, and behavior.

Three Encounters with Christ

Let me leave you with three encounters with Christ.

The first encounter is found in John 6:16-21, where Jesus Walks on Water. Jesus sends the disciples on ahead across the sea while He stays on the mountain to pray. V.18 tells us,

"... the sea began to be stirred up because a strong wind was blowing." Jesus sent them into the storm, but not as punishment for their disobedience. Because they were obedient, they got into the boat. He then came to them, walking on the water, getting his feet wet, and getting into the boat with them. This is the God-who-walks-alongside. Sometimes we see Jesus in the faces of those He uses to walk alongside of us. He walks alongside of us because He loves us.

In Luke 24:13-25, we find the second encounter in a passage that is called the Walk to Emmaus. Two disciples encounter the risen Jesus but do not recognize Him until, in Communion, He breaks the bread. They say, "Were not our hearts burning within us?" He shows us who He is: His identity, His presence, and His peace. Sometimes we encounter Jesus through the means of grace: among them, reading the Bible, prayers, Bible study, Communion, and fasting. But also, taking a walk, gardening, driving, being with our animals, washing dishes ... and more.

The third encounter is recorded in Acts 9:1-19, commonly called the Damascus Road Experience, or as I call it, the Walk to Damascus. In this passage, Paul, "... still breathing threats and murder against the disciples of the Lord," is on a trip to Damascus to arrest Christ-followers when he is blinded by a light and hears God. Paul says, "Who are you, Lord?" I imagine that at that moment, Paul knew who he was addressing and may have asked this question stutteringly. The Lord reveals who He is: His identity, His presence, and His power. Sometimes it is in the breaking of bread. Sometimes it is in the breaking of a spirit. Sometimes it takes a kick in the backside to get our attention.

Shining the Truth, the Light of Christ, into our lives reveals many things: confirmation, affirmation, confrontation. Being confronted with the reality of our actions ... and their consequences, as well as uncovering the lies that we thought were true: power, money, fame, and even religion. What religion? Religion that is tied to meaningless, worshipless ritual as opposed to a vibrant personal faith, a faith in Christ. These lies are Satan's tools because they are idols, false gods. A life built on and in these proves empty, unfulfilling, and unsatisfying. No one, at the end of their life, declares, "Oh, I wish I had spent more time at the office!"

This is certain: however Jesus reveals Himself, it is done in love, a sacrificial love. The world thinks it can put off Jesus, postpone the End of Days, and it lives for and worships the moment. One way or another, we will meet Jesus. One day, sooner or later, we will meet Jesus. We will all, each of us, acknowledge Jesus Christ as the Son of God, Lord and Master, the Lamb of God.

Remembering how and where He reached us, what He has cleansed us from, and trusting Him to lead us…wherever: that is the path to Life! Life, both in Heaven and here. Knowing He loved us first motivates us into serving Him through serving others. And in the serving is the blessing.

Appendix A

The 12 Steps of AA

AA's 12-Step approach follows a set of guidelines designed as "steps" toward recovery, and members can revisit these steps at any time. The 12 Steps are:

1. We admitted we were powerless over alcohol—that our lives had become unmanageable.

2. Came to believe that a Power greater than ourselves could restore us to sanity.

3. Made a decision to turn our will and our lives over to the care of God as we understood Him.

4. Made a searching and fearless moral inventory of ourselves.

5. Admitted to God, to ourselves, and to another human being the exact nature of our wrongs.

6. Were entirely ready to have God remove all these defects of character.

7. Humbly asked Him to remove our shortcomings.

8. Made a list of all persons we had harmed, and became willing to make amends to them all.

9. Made direct amends to such people wherever possible, except when to do so would injure them or others.

10. Continued to take personal inventory and when we were wrong promptly admitted it.

11. Sought through prayer and meditation to improve our conscious contact with God, as we understood Him, praying only for knowledge of His will for us and the power to carry that out.

12. Having had a spiritual awakening as the result of these Steps, we tried to carry this message to alcoholics, and to practice these principles in all our affairs.

Appendix A

Name: _____   Today's Date: _____

Post-Traumatic Stress Disorder*

Instructions. Use checks (✓) to indicate how much you have experienced each symptom in the past week, including today. **Please answer all the items.**

Rating scale: 0—Not at all | 1—Somewhat | 2—Moderately | 3—A lot | 4—Extremely

Category A: Exposure to a Traumatic Event

	0	1	2	3	4
1. Have you experienced or witnessed a traumatic event such as death, serious injury, or a threat to your life or someone else's?					
2. Did you feel intensely afraid, helpless or horrified when this event occurred?					

Category B: Persistent Memories

	0	1	2	3	4
3. Do upsetting memories of the traumatic event come into your mind over and over?					
4. Do you have upsetting dreams about the traumatic event?					
5. Do you have flashbacks and feel like the event is happening again?					
6. Do you get upset when you think about the event or when you're reminded of it?					
7. Do you have strong physical sensations, such as increased heart rate or sweating, when you're reminded about the event?					

Category C: Avoidance

	0	1	2	3	4
8. Do you avoid thinking or talking about the event?					
9. Do you avoid people, things, or places that remind you of the event?					
10. Are there parts of the event you can't recall?					
11. Have you lost interest in life?					
12. Do you often feel isolated or alienated from other people?					
13. Do you feel numb or unable to experience love, pleasure and happiness?					
14. Do you often feel like you have no future?					

Category D: Agitation and Arousal

	0	1	2	3	4
15. Do you have trouble sleeping?					
16. Do you get irritable or have angry outbursts?					
17. Do you have trouble concentrating?					
18. Are you always on the lookout to make sure you don't experience the event again?					
19. Do you get startled easily?					

Category E: Distress

	0	1	2	3	4
20. How much do your reactions to this event interfere with your life?					

Category F: Duration

	Years	Months
How long have you experienced these kinds of symptoms? If unsure, just estimate.		

Use checks (✓) to indicate the types of traumatic event(s) you experienced, with the dates.

Traumatic Event	(✓)	Date	Traumatic Event	(✓)	Date
Accident			War trauma		
Natural disaster			Physical assault		
Sexual assault			Torture		
Being in prison			Serious illness		
Other event (describe):					

157

APPENDIX B BURNS PTSD SCALE

How to Score the 20-Item PTSD Scale[*]

Many symptoms on this scale are *not* specific to PTSD, and are often observed in other Axis I or Axis II disorders. I've listed these non-specific symptoms in the following table.

Keep this in mind when you interpret the scores on the test. For example, a severely depressed individual could easily score 24 on this test, and still have no absolutely *no* history or symptoms suggesting PTSD. Someone who is depressed, anxious and angry could score a 36 or higher, and still have no specific symptoms of PTSD.

Disorder	Scale items
Depression	11, 12, 13, 14, 15, 17, 20
Anxiety	12, 15, 17, 19, 20
Anger, relationship problems, mania, or personality disorders (such as BPD)	12, 13, 16, 20

Why is this? Is there something wrong with this PTSD test? Yes there is.

The test is modeled after the DSM-IV Diagnostic Criteria for PTSD and is intended to assist you in screening for this disorder. However, the DSM-IV criteria contain approximately 11 symptoms that are reasonably specific to PTSD and 9 symptoms that are rather non-specific, as you've just seen. Any test that maps onto these criteria will necessarily be flawed, because the DSM-IV criteria for PTSD are flawed.

The grouping categories don't always make much sense, either, and they would not hold up in a factor analysis. For example, item 7 seems to belong in category D, since it reflects agitation. However, DSM-IV places it in the Persistent Memories category, and that's why you'll find it there.

You will find many other inconsistencies if you examine the test critically. However, the goal was not to create the finest possible PTSD test, but rather to create a user-friendly test that will make it easy for you to assess the DSM-IV criteria quickly and accurately.

Score	Interpretation	Comment
0 – 2	Few or no symptoms of PTSD	Nine of the 20 test items assess symptoms of depression, anxiety, and anger, and are not specific to PTSD. Scores in this range may result from other disorders. The non-specific symptoms may inflate the total score.
3 – 5	Few, if any, symptoms of PTSD	
6 – 10	Borderline symptoms of PTSD	
11 – 20	Mild symptoms of PTSD	
21 – 40	Moderate symptoms of PTSD	
41 – 60	Severe symptoms of PTSD	Scores this high are likely to be due to PTSD.
61 – 80	Extreme symptoms of PTSD	

PCL-5

Instructions: Below is a list of problems that people sometimes have in response to a very stressful experience. Please read each problem carefully and then circle one of the numbers to the right to indicate how much you have been bothered by that problem <u>in the past month</u>.

In the past month, how much were you bothered by:	Not at all	A little bit	Moderately	Quite a bit	Extremely
1. Repeated, disturbing, and unwanted memories of the stressful experience?	0	1	2	3	4
2. Repeated, disturbing dreams of the stressful experience?	0	1	2	3	4
3. Suddenly feeling or acting as if the stressful experience were actually happening again (as if you were actually back there reliving it)?	0	1	2	3	4
4. Feeling very upset when something reminded you of the stressful experience?	0	1	2	3	4
5. Having strong physical reactions when something reminded you of the stressful experience (for example, heart pounding, trouble breathing, sweating)?	0	1	2	3	4
6. Avoiding memories, thoughts, or feelings related to the stressful experience?	0	1	2	3	4
7. Avoiding external reminders of the stressful experience (for example, people, places, conversations, activities, objects, or situations)?	0	1	2	3	4
8. Trouble remembering important parts of the stressful experience?	0	1	2	3	4
9. Having strong negative beliefs about yourself, other people, or the world (for example, having thoughts such as: I am bad, there is something seriously wrong with me, no one can be trusted, the world is completely dangerous)?	0	1	2	3	4
10. Blaming yourself or someone else for the stressful experience or what happened after it?	0	1	2	3	4
11. Having strong negative feelings such as fear, horror, anger, guilt, or shame?	0	1	2	3	4
12. Loss of interest in activities that you used to enjoy?	0	1	2	3	4
13. Feeling distant or cut off from other people?	0	1	2	3	4
14. Trouble experiencing positive feelings (for example, being unable to feel happiness or have loving feelings for people close to you)?	0	1	2	3	4
15. Irritable behavior, angry outbursts, or acting aggressively?	0	1	2	3	4
16. Taking too many risks or doing things that could cause you harm?	0	1	2	3	4
17. Being "superalert" or watchful or on guard?	0	1	2	3	4
18. Feeling jumpy or easily startled?	0	1	2	3	4
19. Having difficulty concentrating?	0	1	2	3	4
20. Trouble falling or staying asleep?	0	1	2	3	4

PCL-5 (8/14/2013) Weathers, Litz, Keane, Palmieri, Marx, & Schnurr -- National Center for PTSD

Appendix C PCL-5 PTSD Checklist

The PCL can be scored in several ways:

- A total symptom severity score (range = 17-85) can be obtained by summing the scores from each of the 17 items that have response options ranging from 1 to 5.

- The gold standard for diagnosing PTSD is a structured clinical interview such as the Clinician-Administered PTSD Scale (CAPS). When necessary, the PCL can be scored to provide a presumptive diagnosis. This has been done in three ways:

  (1) determine whether an individual meets DSM-IV symptom criteria as defined by at least 1 B item (questions 1-5), 3 C items (questions 6-12), and at least 2 D items (questions 13-17). Symptoms rated as "Moderately" or above (responses 3 through 5 on individual items) are counted as present.

  (2) determine whether the total severity score exceeds a given normative threshold

(3) combine methods (1) and (2) to ensure that an individual meets both the symptom pattern and severity threshold.

Choosing a cut-point score

Factors to be considered when choosing a PCL cut-point score include:

- The goal of the assessment: A lower cut-point is considered when screening for PTSD or when it is desirable to maximize detection of possible cases. A higher cut-point is considered when informing diagnosis or to minimize false positives.

- The prevalence of PTSD in the target setting: Generally, the lower the prevalence of PTSD in a given setting, the lower the optimal cut-point. In settings with expected high rates of PTSD, such as specialty mental health clinics, consider a higher cut-point. In settings with expected low rates of PTSD, such as primary care clinics or circumstances in which patients are reluctant to disclose mental health problems, consider a lower cut- point.

Below are suggested cut-point ranges based on prevalence and setting characteristics. Consider scores on the low end of the range if the goal is to screen for PTSD. Consider scores on the high end of the range if the goal is to aid in diagnosis of PTSD.

Suggested PCL cut-point scores

Estimated Prevalence of PTSD
Suggested PCL Cut-Point Scores Below 15%   30-35
(Civilian primary care, Department of Defense screening)

16-39%   36-44
(VA primary care, specialized medical clinics such as TBI or pain)

Above 40%   45-50
(Specialty mental health clinic)

Note. These recommendations are general and approximate, and are not intended to be used for legal or policy purposes. Research is needed to establish optimal cut-point scores for a specific application.

Measuring change

Good clinical practice often involves monitoring patient progress. Evidence suggests that a 5-10 point change is reliable (i.e., not due to chance) and a 10-20 point change is clinically meaningful (Monson et al., 2008). Therefore, we recommend using 5 points as a minimum threshold for determining whether an individual has responded to treatment and 10 points as a minimum threshold for determining whether the improvement is clinically meaningful.

BIBLIOGRAPHY

Adsit, Chris, *The Combat Trauma Healing Manual: Christ-Centered Solutions for Combat Trauma*. Newport News, VA: Military Ministry Press, 2007.

Alcoholics Anonymous, *Twelve Steps and Twelve Traditions*, NY: Alcoholics Anonymous World Services, Inc., 2009.

American Catholic, "The Sacraments: Reconciliation," http://www.americancatholic.org/features/special/default.aspx-?id=32,(Acessed March 23, 2013.)

American Heritage Dictionary, 2d College ed. Boston: Houghton Mifflin, 1982.

American Psychiatric Association, *Diagnostic and Statistical Manual of Mental Disorders*, 4th ed., Text Revision, (DSM-IV-TR) (1), Arlington, VA: American Psychiatric Publishing, 2000.

American Psychiatric Association, *Diagnostic and Statistical Manual of Mental Disorders*, 5th ed., (DSM-5). Arlington, VA: American Psychiatric Publishing, 2013.

Army Guide, https://www.armystudyguide.com/content/army board study guide topics/code of conduct/the-code-of-conduct.shtml. (Accessed September 1, 2022.)

Baker, John, *Your First Step to Celebrate Victory: How God Can Heal Your Life.* Grand Rapids, MI: Zondervan, 2012.

Belgum, David, *Guilt: Where Psychology and Religion Meet.* Englewood Cliffs, NJ: Prentice-Hall, 1963.

Biggar, Nigel, *In Defence of War.* Oxford: Oxford University Press, 2014.

Bonhoeffer, Dietrich, *Letters and Papers from Prison: The Enlarged Edition.* NY: SCM Press, 1971.

Book of Common Prayer, http://www.bcponline.org/,(Accessed March 23, 2013.)

Bowman, George W. III, *The Dynamics of Confession.* Richmond, VA: John Knox Press, 1969.

Brock, Rita Nakashima, and Gabriella Lettini, *Soul Repair: Recovering from Moral Injury after War.* Boston: Beacon Press, 2012.

Brown, Pamela J., "Outcome in Female Patients with both Substance Use and Post- Traumatic Stress Disorders. *Alcoholism Treatment Quarterly*, 3, Vol 18,(2000):127-135.

Brown, Pamela J. and Paige C. Ouimette, "Introduction to the Special Section on Substance Use Disorder and Posttraumatic Stress Disorder Comorbidity." *Psychology of Addictive Behaviors*, 2, Vol 13,(1999):75-77.

Brown, Pamela J., Robert L. Stout, and Timothy Mueller, "Posttraumatic Stress Disorder and Substance Abuse Relapse Among Women: A Pilot Study." *Psychology of Addictive Behaviors*, 2, Vol 10, (1996):124-128.

Brown, Pamela J., Robert L. Stout, and Jolyne Gannon-Rowley, "Substance Use Disorder-PTSD Comorbidity: Patients' Perceptions of Symptom Interplay and Treatment Issues." *Journal of Substance Abuse Treatment*, 5, Vol 15, (1998):445-448.

Brueggemann, Walter, *Hope within History*. Westminster: John Knox Press, 1987.

Brueggemann, Walter, *The Prophetic Imagination*. 2nd ed. Minneapolis: Fortress Press, 2001.

Budden, Ashwin, "The Role of Shame in Posttraumatic Stress Disorder: A Proposal for a Socio-Emotional Model for DSM-V," *Social Science and Medicine*, Vol 69, (2009): 1032-1039.

Certain, Robert, *Unchained Eagle: From Prisoner of War to Prisoner of Christ*. Palm Springs, CA: ETC Publications, 2003.

Clark, Allen B., *Wounded Soldier, Healing Warrior*. St Paul, MN: Zenith Press, 2007.

Cuilleanain, Donal O., *A Guidebook for Confession: The Sacrament of Reconciliation*. Princeton: Scepter Publishers, 1996.

Curington, Steve, "The Ten Principles," Reformers Unanimous Christian Addiction Recovery Program, http://reformersre-covery.com/10principles,(Accessed June 20, 2014.)

Dein, Simon, "Religion, Spirituality, and Mental Health: Theoretical and Clinical Perspectives," *Psychiatric Times*, 1, Vol 27, (January 2010): 1-7.

Doehring, Carrie, *Internal Desecration: Traumatization and Representations of God*. Lanham, MD: University Press of America, 1991.

Dohrenwend, Bruce P., Thomas J. Yager, Melanie M. Wall, Ben G. Adams, "The Roles of Combat Exposure, Personal Vulnerability, and Involvement in Harm to Civilians or Prisoners in Vietnam War-Related Posttraumatic Stress Disorder," *Clinical Psychological Science*, 10, Vol 20, (2012): 1-16.

Dolan, Joshua, "Treatment of Dual Diagnosis Post Traumatic Stress Disorder and Substance Use Disorders: A Meta-Analysis." (2012). Marquette University Dissertations (2009 -). Paper 177. http://epublications.marquette.edu/dissertations_mu/177,(Accessed September 25, 2014.)

Drescher, Kent D., telephonic interview by author, National Center for PTSD, Menlo Park, CA, February 8, 2013.

Dyslin, Christopher W., "The Power of Powerlessness: The Role of Spiritual Surrender and Interpersonal Confession in the Treatment of Addiction," *Journal of Psychology and Christianity*, 1, Vol 27, (Spring 2008): 41-55.

Exline, Julie J., Ann M. Yali, and Marci Lobel, "When God Disappoints: Difficulty Forgiving God and its Role in Negative Emotion," *Journal of Health Psychology*, 3, Vol 4, (1999): 365-379.

Fontana, Alan and Robert Rosenheck, "Trauma, Change in Strength of Religious Faith, and Mental Health Service Use Among Veterans Treated for PTSD," *The Journal of Nervous and Mental Disease*, 9, Volume 192,(September 2004): 579-584.

Forest, Jim, *Confession: Doorway to Forgiveness*. Maryknoll, NY: Orbis Books, 2002. Frankl, Victor E., *Man's Search for Meaning*. Boston: Beacon Press, 2006.

Gignilliat, Mark, "Ora et Labora: Barth's Forgotten Hermeneutical Principle," *Expository Times*, 6, Vol 120, (March 2009): 277-281.

Graham, Larry K., "Trauma and Transformation at Ground Zero: A Pastoral Theology," *Journal of Pastoral Theology*, 2, Vol 22, (Winter 2012): 7-1-7-9.

Grassman, Deborah, "Wounded Warriors: Their Last Battle," Conference presentation, Midland, TX, March 6, 2015.

Grossman, Dave, *On Killing: The Psychological Cost of Learning to Kill in War and Society*. NY: Back Bay Books, 2009.

Hall, Julie H., and Frank D. Fingham, "Self-Forgiveness: The Stepchild of Forgiveness Research," *Journal of Social and Clinical Psychology*, 5, Vol 24, (2005): 621-637.

Harris, Russ, *ACT Made Simple: An Easy-to-Read Primer on Acceptance and Commitment Therapy*. Oakland, CA: New Harbinger Publications, 2009.

Hays, Richard B., *The Moral Vision of the New Testament*. NY: Harper Collins, 1996.

Herman, Judith, *Trauma and Recovery: The Aftermath of Violence – From Domestic Abuse to Political Terror*. NY: Basic Books, 1992, 1997.

Hermann, Barbara A., Jessica L. Hamblen, Nancy C. Bernady, and Paula P. Schnurr, "Evaluating the Evidence for PTSD-SUD Treatment," In *Trauma and Substance Abuse: Causes, Consequences, and Treatment of Comorbid Disorders*, ed. Paige Ouimette and Pamela P. Read. 2nd ed. Washington, D.C.: American Psychological Association, 2014.

Hirt-Manheimer, Aron, "Against Indifference: A Conversation with Elie Wiesel," *Reform Judaism Online*. http://reform-judaismmag.org/Articles/index.cfm?id=1074&go-back=%2Egde_108049_member_5909686850427043843, (Accessed August 26, 2014.)

Holman Christian Standard Bible (HCSB), Holman Bible Publishers, 2009.

Hruska, Bryce and Douglas Delahanty, "PTSD-SUD Biological Mechanisms: Self- Medication and Beyond," In *Trauma and Substance Abuse: Causes, Consequences, and Treatment of Comorbid Disorders*, ed. Paige Ouimette and Pamela P. Read. 2nd ed. Washington, D.C.: American Psychological Association, 2014.

Jones, Cory, "Repairing the Altar in the Church," http://nmi.nazarene.org/workshops/Files/Workshops/106/106JonesRepairingtheAltar20 13.pdf, (Accessed April 17, 2015).

King James Version (KJV), Public Domain.

Litz, Brett T., Nathan Stein, Eileen Delaney, Leslie Lebowitz, William P. Nash, Caroline Silva, and Shira Maguen, "Moral Injury and Moral Repair in War Veterans: A Preliminary Model and Intervention Strategy," *Clinical Psychology Review*, 29, (2009): 695-706.

Maguen, Shira and Brett Litz, "Moral Injury in the Context of War," Department of Veterans Affairs, National Center for PTSD. Washington, D.C. http://www.ptsd.va.gov/professional/pages/moral_injury_at_war.asp,(Accessed January 25, 2013.

McLeod, D. Scott, Karestan C. Koenen, Joanne M. Meyer, Michael J. Lyons, Seth Eisen, William True, and Jack Goldberg, "Genetic and Environmental Influences on the Relationship among Combat Exposure, Posttraumatic Stress Disorder Symptoms, and Alcohol Use." *Journal of Traumatic Stress*, 2 Vol 14, (2001): 259-275.

McManus, Kathleen, "Suffering in the Theology of Edward Schillebeeckx," *Theological Studies* 60, (1999): 476-491.

Middendorf, Jesse C., *Church Rituals Handbook*. 2ⁿᵈ ed. Church of the Nazarene, Kansas City: Beacon Hill Press, 2009.

Moltmann, Jürgen, *The Crucified God: the Cross of Christ As the Foundation and Criticism of Christian Theology*. Minneapolis, MN: Augsburg Fortress Publishers, 1983.

Morrison, Jay A., Erin C. Berenz, and Scott E. Coffey, "Exposure-Based, Trauma- Focused Treatment for Comorbid PTSD-SUD," In *Trauma and Substance Abuse: Causes, Consequences, and Treatment of Comorbid Disorders*, ed. Paige Ouimette and Pamela P. Read. 2nd ed. Washington, D.C.: American Psychological Association, 2014.

Moschella, Mary Clark, *Ethnography as a Pastoral Practice: an Introduction*. Cleveland: The Pilgrim Press, 2008.

Murray-Swank, Aaron, Kelly M. McConnell, and Kenneth I. Pargament, "Understanding Spiritual Confession: A Review and Theoretical Synthesis," *Mental Health, Religion, and Culture*, 3, Vol 10 (May 2007): 275-291.

Myers, Isabel Briggs and Mary H. McCaulley, *Manual: A Guide to the Development and Use of the Myers-Briggs Temperament Indicator*. Palo Alto, CA: Consulting Psychologists Press, 1985.

Najavits, Lisa M., "Creating Change: A New Past-Focused Model for Trauma and Substance Abuse," In *Trauma and Substance Abuse: Causes, Consequences, and Treatment of Comorbid Disorders*. ed. Paige Ouimette and Pamela P. Read, 2nd ed. Washington, D.C.: American Psychological Association, 2014.

Najavits, Lisa M. and Kay M. Johnson, "Pilot Study of Creating Change, a New Past Focused Model for PTSD and Substance Abuse," *The American Journal on Addictions*, XX, (2014): 1–8.

Nash, William P., Lillian Krantz, Nathan Stein, Richard J. Westphal, and Bret Litz, "Comprehensive Soldier Fitness, Battlemind, and the Stress Continuum Model: Military Organizational Approaches to Prevention," *In Caring for Veterans with Deployment- Related Stress Disorders: Iraq, Afghanistan, and Beyond*. ed. Josef I. Ruzek, Paula P. Schnurr, Jennifer J. Vasterling, and Matthew J. Friedman. Washington, D.C.: American Psychological Association, 2011.

National Center for PTSD, "Spirituality and Trauma: Professionals Working Together" Department of Veterans Affairs, National Center for PTSD. Washington, D.C. http://www.ptsd.va.gov/professiona/pages/fs-spirituoltiy.asp,(Accessed January 25, 2013.)

New Revised Standard Version Bible (NRSV), National Council of the Churches of Christ in the United States of America, 1989.

Pitchford, Daniel, "An Existential Study of Iraq Veterans' Traumatizing Experiences," UMI: 3339401, San Francisco: Saybrook Graduate School and Research Center, 2008.

Rothbaum, Barbara O., Maryrose Gerardi, Bekh Bradley, and Matthew J. Friedman, "Evidence-Based Treatments for Posttraumatic Stress Disorder in Operation Enduring Freedom and Operation Iraqi Freedom Military Personnel," In *Caring for Veterans with Deployment-Related Stress Disorders: Iraq, Afghanistan, and Beyond.* ed. Josef I. Ruzek, Paula P. Schnurr, Jennifer J. Vasterling, and Matthew J. Friedman. Washington, D.C.: American Psychological Association, 2011.

Ruzek, Joseph I. and Patricia Watson, "Early Intervention to Prevent PTSD and Other Trauma-Related Problems," *NC-PTSD Quarterly*, 4, Vol 12 (Fall 2001): 1-3.

Shay, Jonathan, *Achilles in Vietnam: Combat Trauma and the Undoing of Character.* NY: Simon and Schuster, 1995.

Sites, Kevin, *The Things They Cannot Say: Stories Soldiers Won't Tell You about What They've Seen, Done or Failed to Do in War.* NY: Harper Collins Publishers, 2013.

Smith, Martin L., *Reconciliation: Preparing for Confession in the Episcopal Church.* Cambridge, MA: Cowley Publications, 1985.

Tanielian, Terri and Lisa H. Jaycox, editors, "Invisible Wounds of War: Psychological and Cognitive Injuries, Their Consequences, and Services to Assist Recovery." xxi, http://www.rand.org/content/dam/rand/pubs/monographs/2008/RAND_MG720.pdf, (Accessed November 4, 2014.)

Ter Kuile, Hagar and Thomas Ehring, "Predictors of Changes in Religiosity After Trauma: Trauma Religiosity, and Posttraumatic Stress Disorder," *Psychological Trauma: Theory, Research, Practice, and Policy*, 4, Vol 6, (2014): 353-360.

Tick, Edward, *War and the Soul: Healing Our Nation's Veterans from Post-Traumatic Stress Disorder*. Wheaton, IL: Quest Books, 2005.

Tillar, Elizabeth K., "Suffering for Others in the Theology of Edward Schillebeeckx," PhD dissertation, January 1, 2000. ETD Collection for Fordham University. Paper AA19955973. http://fordham.bepress.com/dissertations/AA19955973,(Accessed July 9, 2012.)

Van Dyke, Michael, *Radical Integrity: The Story of Dietrich Bonhoeffer.* Uhrichsville, OH: Barbour Publishing, 2001.

Vasterling, Jennifer J., Erin S. Daly, and Matthew J. Friedman, "Posttraumatic Stress Reactions Over Time: The Battlefield, Homecoming, and Long-Term Course," In *Caring for Veterans with Deployment-Related Stress Disorders: Iraq, Afghanistan, and Beyond,* ed. Ruzek, Joseph I., Paula P. Schnurr, Jennifer J. Vasterling, and Matthew J. Friedman. Washington, D.C.: American Psychological Association, 2011.

Wasdin, Howard and Joel Kilpatrick, *The Last Rescue: How Faith and Love Saved a Navy SEAL Sniper*. Nashville, TN: Nelson Books, 2014.

Wiesel, Eli, *Night*. NY: Bantam Books, 1982.

Williams, Ken, "Toward a Biblical Theology of Suffering," http://www.google.com/search/q=theology+of+suffering&hl=en&safe=active&gbv=2& gs-l=serp.1.0.0j0i303l-3j0i22l2.10110.10110.0.13922.1.1.0.0.0.219.219.2-1.1.0.0.0 FeVvKueK4VM&oq=theology=of+suffering,(Accessed July 10, 2012.)

Wood, David, "Iraq, Afghanistan War Veterans Struggle With Combat Trauma," http://www.huffingtonpost.com/2012/07/04/iraq-afghanistan-war-veterans-combat- trauma n 1645701.html. Posted July 4, 2012, (Accessed July 9, 2012.)

Worthington, Everett L. and Diane Langberg, "Religious Considerations and Self- Forgiveness in Treating Complex Trauma and Moral Injury in Present and Former Soldiers," *Journal of Psychology and Theology*, 4, Vol 40, (2012): 274-288.

WORKS CONSULTED

Askay, Shelley W. and Gina Magyar-Russell, "Posttraumatic Growth and Spirituality in Burn Recovery," *International Review of Psychiatry*, 6 Vol 21, (December 2009): 570-579.

Baker, John, *Life's Healing Choices; Freedom from Your Hurts, Hang-ups, and Habits*. NY: Howard Books, 2007.

Berg, Gary, "The Relationship between Spiritual Distress, PTSD, and Depression in Vietnam Combat Veterans," *Journal of Pastoral Care*, 1-2, Vol 65, (Spring-Summer 2011): 1-11.

Bray, Peter, "A Broader Framework for Exploring the Influence of Spiritual Experience in the Wake of Stressful Life Events; Examining Connections Between Posttraumatic Growth and Psycho-Spiritual Transformation," *Mental Health, Religion, and Culture*,3, Vol 13 (April 2010): 293-308.

Brady, Kathleen T., "Comorbid Posttraumatic Stress Disorder and Substance Use Disorders." *Psychiatric Annals*, 5, Vol. 31, (2001):313-319.

Brewin, Chris R., Ruth A Lanius, Andrei Novac, Ulrich Schnyder, and Sandro Galea, "Reformulating PTSD for

DSM-V: Life after Criterion A," *Journal of Traumatic Stress*, 5, Vol 22, (October 2009): 366-373.

Chandler, Emily, "Religious and Spiritual Issues in DSM-5: Matters of the Mind and Searching of the Soul," *Issues in Mental Health Nursing*, Vol 33 (2012): 577-582.

Department of Defense Center of Excellence (DCoE) for Psychological Health and Traumatic Brain Injury, http://dcoe.mil.

Delanty, Douglas L., Holly B. Herberman, Karrie J. Craig, Michele C. Hayward, Carol S. Fullerton, Robert J. Ursano, and Andrew Baum, "Acute and Chronic Distress and Posttraumatic Stress Disorder as a Function of Responsibility for Serious Motor Vehicle Accidents," *Journal of Consulting and Clinical Psychology*, 4, Vol 65, (1997): 560-567.

Donovan, Jane, "Battle Scars," *The Christian Century*, 3, Vol 129, (2012): 34-36

Drescher, Kent D. and David W. Foy, "When Horror and Loss Intersect: Traumatic Experiences and Traumatic Bereavement," *Pastoral Psychology*, 2, Vol 59, (April 2010): 147-158.

Drescher, Kent D., David W. Foy, Caroline Kelly, Anna Leshner, Kerrie Schutz, and Brett Litz, "An Exploration of the Viability and Usefulness of the Construct of Moral Injury in War Veterans," *Traumatology*, 10 , Vol 20, (2011): 1-6.

Eynon, Shane, "Combat Trauma, Moral Injuries, and Suicide: What Works in the Trenches?" *LinkedInPulse*, April 13, 2015.

Jacobsen, Leslie K., Steven M. Southwick, and Thomas R. Kosten, "Substance Use Disorders in Patients with Posttraumatic Stress Disorder: A Review of the Literature." *American Journal of Psychiatry*, 8, Vol 158, (2001):1184-1190.

Kübler-Ross, Elisabeth, *On Death & Dying*. NY: Simon & Schuster/Touchstone, 1969.

Lewis, James M., "Pastoral Assessment in Hospital Ministry: A Conversational Approach," *Chaplaincy Today*, 2, Volume 18, (Autumn/Winter 2002): 5-13.

Maguen, Shira and Brett Litz, "Moral Injury in the Veterans of War," *PTSD Research Quarterly*, 1, Vol 23, (2012): 1-6.

Myers, Gary E. and Stephen Roberts, eds, *An Invitation to Chaplaincy Research*. http://www.healthcarechaplaincy.org/docs/publications/templeton_research/hcc_researc h_handbook_final.pdf,(Accessed November 6, 2014.)

National Institutes of Health, "Post-Traumatic Stress Disorder (PTSD)," US Department of Health and Human Services, National Institutes of Health. Washington, D.C.: Government Printing Office.

Sensing, Tim, *Qualitative Research: A Multi-Methods Approach to Projects for Doctor of Ministry Theses*. Eugene, OR: Wipf & Stock Publishers, 2011.

Sonne, Susan C., Sudie E. Back, Claudia Diaz Zuniga, Carrie E. Randall, and Kathleen T. Brady, "Gender Differences in Individuals with Comorbid Alcohol Dependence and Posttraumatic Stress Disorder." *Drug and Alcohol Dependence*, 63(suppl.1),(2001):s9.

Stake, Robert E., *The Art of Case Study Research*. Thousand Oaks: Sage Publications, 1995.

Swales, Pamela, "Coping with Traumatic Stress Reactions: A National Center for PTSD Fact Sheet," Department of Veterans Affairs, National Center for PTSD. Washington, D.C.: Government Printing Office. Foy, David W., Kent D. Drescher, and Mark W. Smith, "Addressing Religion and Spirituality in Military Settings and Veterans' Services," In *APA Handbook of Psychology, Religion, and Spirituality*, Arlington, VA: American Psychiatric Publishing, 2013, 561-576.

Grassman, Deborah L., *The Hero Within: Redeeming the Destiny We Were Born to Fulfill*. St Petersburg, FL: Vandamere Press, 2012. Grassman, Deborah, www.soulinjury.org.

HealthCare Chaplaincy Network's Chaplain Care for Veterans, http://www.chaplaincareforveterans.org/.

Jacob, Mel, "Post-Traumatic Stress Disorder: Facing Futility In and After Vietnam," *Currents in Theology and Mission*, 5, Vol 10, (October 1983): 291-298.

McConnell, John M., "Perceived Forgiveness from God and Self-Forgiveness," *Journal of Psychology and Christianity*, 1, Vol 31, (Spring 2012): 31-39.

McNally, Richard J., "Can we fix PTSD in DSM-V?" *Depression and Anxiety*, 7, Vol 26, (2009): 597-600.

National Center for PTSD (NC-PTSD), www.ptsd.va.gov.

National Institute of Mental Health, "Post-Traumatic Stress Disorder (PTSD)," U.S Department of Health and Human Services, National Institutes of Health, NIH Publication No. 08-6388.

O'Donnell, Meaghan L., "Should A2 be a Diagnostic Requirement for Posttraumatic Stress Disorder in DSM-V?" *Psychiatry Research*, 2-3, Vol 176, (April 2010): 257-260.

Paulson, Daryl S., "The Hard Issues of Life," *Pastoral Psychology*, 5, Vol 49, (2011): 385-394.

Reger, Mark A., Derek J. Smolenski, Nancy A. Skopp, Melinda J. Metzger- Abamukang, Han K. Kang, Tim A. Bullman, Sondra Perdue, Gregory A. Gahm, "Risk of Suicide Among US Military Service Members Following Operation Enduring Freedom or Operation Iraqi Freedom Deployment and Separation From the US Military" *JAMA Psychiatry, jama-psychiatry.com.,* April 1, 2015.

Riedel-Pfaefflin, Ursula and Archie Smith, Jr., "Notes on Diversity and Working Together Across Cultures on Traumatization and Forgiveness: Siblings by Choice," *Pastoral Psychology*, 4, Vol 49 (August 2010): 457-469.

Salem, Benissa, and Jacquelyn H. Flaskerud, "A Closer Look: The Trauma of War and Migration and PTSD," *Issues in Mental Health Nursing*, 3, Vol 32, (August 2010): 184- 186.

Shaw, Annick, Stephen Joseph, and P. Alex Linley, "Religion, Spirituality, and Posttraumatic Growth: a Systematic Review," *Mental Health, Religion, and Culture*, 1, Vol 8, (March 2005): 1-11.

Stine, Oscar C., "A Jungian Interpretation of Spiritual Injury," *The Journal of Pastoral Care and Counseling*, 3, Vol 62, (Fall 2008): 287-288.

Van Dahlen, Barbara, "Killing as an Option," Battleland, TIME.com, http://battleland.blogs.time.com/2012/07/18/killing-as-an-option/,(Accessed June 26, 2012).

Yan, Grace W., "Finding Hope in Pandora's Box: A Clinician's Perspective on Moral Injury," *PlainViews*, 7, Vol 9, (May 2, 2012):1-3.

Zoellner, Tanja, Sirko Rabe, Anke Karl, and Andreas Maercker, "Postraumatic Growth in Accident Survivors: Openness and Optimism as Predictors of its Constructive or Illusory Sides," *Journal of Clinical Psychology*, 3, Vol 64, (March 2008): 245-263.